DATE DUE

NO 2 7'00			
AP 7'03			
AP 8'03			

DEMCO 38-296

Working Sober

Inside an Emotional Health Program: A Field Study of Workplace Assistance for Troubled Employees

Strategies for Employee Assistance Programs: The Crucial Balance (by William J. Sonnenstuhl and Harrison M. Trice)

Member Assistance Programs in the Workplace: The Role of Labor in the Prevention and Treatment of Substance Abuse (by Samuel B. Bacharach, Peter Bamberger, and William J. Sonnenstuhl)

Working Sober

~ *The Transformation of an*
Occupational Drinking Culture

WILLIAM J. SONNENSTUHL

ILR PRESS *an imprint of*
CORNELL UNIVERSITY PRESS
ITHACA AND LONDON

First published 1996 by ILR Press / Cornell University Press.

Printed in the United States of America

⊗ The paper in this book meets the minimum requirements of the
American National Standard for Information Sciences—Permanence
of Paper for Printed Library Materials, ANSI Z39.48–1984.

Library of Congress Cataloging-in-Publication Data

Sonnenstuhl, William J., 1946–
    Working sober : the transformation of an occupational drinking culture /
William J. Sonnenstuhl.
        p. cm.
    Includes bibliographical references and index.
    ISBN 0–8014–3267–7 (alk. paper). — ISBN 0–8014–8348–4 (alk.
paper)
        1. Alcoholism and employment—United States—Case studies.   2. Sandhogs—
Alcohol use—Social aspects—United States—Case studies.   3. Group identity—
United States—Case studies.   4. Drinking of alcoholic beverages—Social aspects—
United States—Case studies.   I. Title.
HF5549.5.A4S66   1996
331.25'98—dc20   95–43596

Dedicated to the memory of my friends and teachers

R. Brinkley Smithers
and
Harrison M. Trice

Contents

Preface

We are shocked by news reports that attribute work-related accidents, especially those that kill and maim the innocent, to workers' drunkenness because we take it for granted that on-the-job drinking is a thing of the past. We assume this seemingly irrational behavior is the result of workers who suffer from alcoholism rather than entertain the possibility that the workers are conforming to occupational expectations. In this book, I examine the drinking culture of a group of tunnel workers, the sandhogs, in order to generate a grounded substantive theory about the persistence and transformation of intemperate occupational drinking cultures in the American workplace. Some occupations continue to build their sense of community around intemperate drinking rituals that encourage members to drink with one another on and off the job, and these cultures are the eventual object of this study.

Chapter 1 highlights the book's focus on intemperate occupational drinking cultures. Here I illustrate the persistence of those cultures within such occupations as railroading, construction, and the military. I also examine the historical efforts of management and labor to curtail intemperate drinking practices at work. This chapter leaves the reader wondering why these intemperate occupational drinking cultures persist and how they are to be transformed to prevent work-related accidents that can maim and kill workers and innocent bystanders.

In the chapters that follow I address these questions by examining the sandhogs and their changing drinking rituals. Chapter 2 lays out the substantive theory I generated from my study of the sandhogs. I examine my use of the terms *occupational culture* and *occupational community* and their relationship to drinking. Essentially, I argue that intemperate drinking cultures persist because drinking is a ritual that marks the occupational community's boundary and creates a sense of solidarity in members. I also argue that these rituals will not change unless occupational members redefine their relationship to drinking, prevent drinking rituals from marking the community's boundary, and create a sense of solidarity in members. Chapter 3 is an overview of the sandhogs' occupational community that recounts its emergence in the late nineteenth century, growth in the early twentieth century, and recent decline due to economic conditions. In this chapter I also illustrate how certain circumstances (e.g., control over work, dangerous working conditions) lead the sandhogs to construct a closely knit occupational community in which members value their identity as sandhogs, take one another as their primary reference group, and meld their work and leisure lives. In Chapter 4 I demonstrate how the sandhogs' intemperate drinking rituals reinforce this sense of occupational community, and in Chapter 5 I examine the processes by which the sandhogs are transforming their intemperate culture into a temperate or sober one. The primary mechanism for this is their alcoholism program, which is made up of a network of sandhogs who are recovering alcoholics. This transformation process has occurred over the last fifteen to twenty years. Today the sandhogs no longer drink at work and discourage heavy drinking after work as well.

The conceptual framework outlined here was generated from a variety of data sources, including historical accounts of workplace drinking, existing case studies of occupational drinking behavior, and, of course, my study of the sandhogs' intemperate drinking culture. In studying the persistence and transformation of the sandhogs' intemperate drinking culture, I used a number of qualitative methods in order to maximize the discovery process and enable me to understand the meanings that the sandhogs attached to their behavior (Bogdan and Taylor 1975; Schwartz and Jacobs 1979; Whyte

1984; Spradley 1979). I wanted to maximize the discovery process because this was the first time that a researcher had been able to observe directly an occupational community's efforts to transform its intemperate drinking culture; consequently, I wanted to remain as open as possible to any new insights that might arise from my observations. Additionally, I chose to use qualitative methods because they would enable me to understand how members of the occupational community interpreted what they were doing: what meanings they attributed to their behavior and what they expected would happen as a consequence of their behavior. This was important because I wanted to understand their definition of the situation, particularly their concepts of intemperate and temperate drinking behavior.

A number of qualitative methods were used: participant observation, ethnographic interviews, and document analysis. Data from these methods were analyzed by the constant comparative method in order to develop a description of the sandhog drinking culture and its transformation and to generate grounded hypotheses about the processes underlying cultural change (Strauss 1987; Glaser and Strauss 1967; Strauss and Corbin 1990).

The basic tool by which the sandhogs are transforming their intemperate drinking culture is the union's alcoholism program. I was able to negotiate access to the program because the director and his two counselors were anxious to tell labor's side of the alcohol story. Between January 1985 and July 1985, I observed them as they interacted with union officers, stewards, members of the union, members' families, rehabilitation personnel from outside the program, and AA members from inside and outside the union. These observations occurred in a large variety of settings, including the director's and counselors' offices and cars, union work sites, bars frequented by union members, members' homes, open AA meetings, an AA dance, and alcohol and drug treatment programs.

I was able to observe life within the sandhog community as well as the alcoholism program. Although my key informants for understanding the sandhog community were recovering alcoholics (i.e., the director, counselors, and one other sober sandhog), I was able to interact and converse with sandhogs who were not involved with the program. For example, when I accompanied the director and counselors on their visits to the work sites, I was able to interact with a broad range of community members, including those whom the counselors regarded as social drinkers and those whom they considered problem drinkers.

Although I did not interview the managers of the construction companies that employ the sandhogs, I was aware of their support for the sandhogs' efforts to transform their intemperate drinking culture. This was evident in the companies' contributions to the sandhogs' welfare funds, which helped to support the alcoholism program. In addition, the contractors were also active in their trade association's campaign to develop alcoholism programs within the construction trade, pointing to the sandhogs' program as an example of what could be done to curb workplace drinking. Finally, the sandhogs frequently spoke about how the contractors, rather than disciplining workers, encouraged problem drinkers to seek help from the program.

I recorded my observations and conversations in field notes. Some of these were written while I was in the field; the rest were written within twenty-four hours after leaving the field. I analyzed these notes using constant comparative analysis; as insights emerged from the data, I followed them up with additional observations and tape-recorded ethnographic interviews (Spradley 1979) to confirm and fill out my understanding of the meanings that actors attributed to these events. To the best of my knowledge, the field notes that I made could have been written by any similarly situated ethnographer. In order to increase validity, I submitted an earlier draft of the manuscript for this book to the program director and several other sandhogs who suggested specific additions and corrections.

Although I was unable to be in the field with the sandhogs after 1985, I did keep abreast of their fortunes through my key informants. Initially, I was in touch with all four of them; but gradually, their number declined to one, the program director. One counselor died of a cerebral hemorrhage; the other counselor left the sandhogs in order to develop an alcoholism program for another union; and my network informant left to take another job. In the spring of 1992, I conducted a group interview with six sandhogs who were all members of AA. I used this group session to reconfirm my earlier findings and to elaborate on the cultural changes that had been reported to me by my informants. Finally, before submitting the final manuscript to the publisher, I once again visited the sandhogs at their present work site, where I was able to confirm through observation and informal interviews that the sandhogs have made remarkable progress in transforming their drinking culture.

Nevertheless, an important caveat is necessary. As I have noted above, the persistence of intemperate drinking cultures is due to the ability of members to pass on their drinking rituals from one generation to another. As of now, the sandhogs have interrupted that transmission process by recruiting only social drinkers and recovering alcoholics on the gangs and by teaching initiates that one does not have to drink in order to be a sandhog. They now regard their culture as a sober one. Whether this process will continue over many generations remains an empirical question to be investigated. Indeed, the sandhogs are aware that, in order to maintain their sober culture, they must remain vigilant about reinforcing their temperate beliefs so that future generations come to regard them as common sense.

This book has been in the making for a long time, and it has benefited from the encouragement and support I have received from a number of individuals. First, I should like to give a special thanks to the sandhogs who shared their personal experiences with me. Without their help, this book would not have have been possible. I especially thank Richard Fitzsimmons, the sandhogs' business manager; Joseph M., director of the sandhogs' Employee Assistance Program; and George S. and Edward T. for their generous support and encouragement. I also thank my colleagues who read earlier drafts of the manuscript and provided me with feedback. These colleagues include Peter Bamberger, Valerie Kennedy, Bryan Mundell, William Staudenmeier, Jr., Paul Steele, and several anonymous reviewers; all provided me with excellent comments. I should like to acknowledge especially the support and encouragement I received from Samuel Bacharach and Paul Roman, whose critiques of earlier drafts were particularly helpful; the manuscript has benefited greatly from their generous remarks. I also thank Colleen Clauson and Margaret Gleason for their patience and support through the drafting and redrafting process, especially their help with the tedious job of pulling together and organizing the references. In addition, I thank Frances Benson, editor-in-chief of Cornell University Press, for her unwavering support for this project, and Janet Wagner, my wife, for her editorial help.

Finally I should like to acknowledge the special support I received from R. Brinkley Smithers and Harrison Trice, without whom this project would never have been undertaken. In the mid-eighties, Brink Smithers gave Harry Trice and me a small grant to conduct this research. In 1987, Harry and I published an article from our findings, "The Social Construction of Alcohol Problems in a Union's Peer Counseling Program" (Sonnenstuhl and Trice 1987), which is the basis for Chapter 5 of this book. (This material is used here by permission of the *Journal of Drug Issues.*) Brink and Harry were both particularly pleased with these findings because they suggested that, despite the professionalization of alcoholism treatment programs, the traditional message of Alcoholics Anonymous was still very much alive in the American workplace and that it continued to offer working Americans a simple method of controlling drinking problems at work. In 1994, Brink and Harry died. My last conversation with each of them was about the sandhogs and the lessons that they have to teach us about transforming intemperate drinking cultures. Therefore, it is to their memory that I dedicate this book.

WILLIAM J. SONNENSTUHL

Ithaca, New York

Working Sober

1 *Drinking and Work*

*D*isaster overtook the New York Transit Authority's Woodlawn Express at 12:10 A.M. The speeding subway train derailed, smashing into the tunnel wall, sheering off a dozen steel beams, and hurling passengers like rag dolls through the cars. Five were crushed to death; scores suffered broken bones. It was the worst subway disaster in sixty-three years, and it was caused by a drunken motorman. After the crash, the motorman's supervisors and co-workers acknowledged they knew he had been drinking but felt helpless to intervene. Despite the authority's rules against drinking and an employee assistance program for rehabilitating alcoholic workers, the supervisors, who were charged with keeping the trains running, had been uncertain about how to respond. The motorman's co-workers also were reluctant to intervene because they adhered to a code of silence about one another's drinking.

Incidents like the Woodlawn Express accident strike terror in the hearts of Americans, who, since the latter half of the nineteenth century, have generally taken it for granted that drinking and work do not mix and that on-the-job drinking, in particular, is deviant or unacceptable behavior (Gusfield 1991). Indeed, it is difficult for us to comprehend why workers, particularly those responsible for maintaining public safety, continue to drink on the job, risking their own lives as well as those of their co-workers and the public whom they serve. It is also difficult for many of us to comprehend why their supervisors and co-workers would feel uncertain about how to intervene. Yet the media continue to report such horror stories: The Conrail-Amtrak accident at Chase, Maryland, caused by an engineer high on alcohol and drugs; the Exxon Valdez accident attributed to an intoxicated ship captain.[1] While such tragedies make us wonder why workers drink on the job, it is necessary to recognize that, throughout American history, drinking and work practices have been closely entwined and some occupations continue to regard drinking at work as an acceptable practice.

Drinking and Work: Some Occupational Examples

For much of American history, fermented alcoholic beverages such as beer and wine were regarded as healthful beverages, essential for life (Lender and Martin 1987). Men, women, and children consumed them throughout the day. They consumed them with their meals, in the harvest fields, at their work benches, and during their leisure pursuits. In the nineteenth century, as farmers began to seek greater production from their fields and industrial entrepreneurs to seek greater control over their workers, drinking patterns began to change so that most workers eventually came to regard drinking as exclusively a leisure activity (Gusfield 1991). Still, many occupations continued to regard mixing drink and work as customary practice. It is instructive to consider a few such occupations and the extent to which they have retained their drinking customs.

[1] Most studies of occupational drinking practices have failed to examine workers' on-the-job drinking, focusing instead upon their leisure-time activities (Ames 1993). This focus reflects the extent to which the belief that drinking and work do not mix has become institutionalized within the American workplace. That is, even social scientists tend to take it for granted that workers no longer drink at work and thus do not ask questions about such practices. In addition, it is important to note that researchers have only recently begun to do large-scale studies of the variation in alcohol use and abuse across occupations (e.g., Parker and Harford 1992; Stinson, DeBakey, and Steffens 1992). These studies suggest that popular opinion about which occupations are most likely to abuse alcohol do not accord well with actual prevalence rates.

Drinking has always been closely associated with the work of craftsmen. Staudenmeier (1985: 20–21) describes the extent to which drinking was integrated into the construction of the first stone government building in Albany, New York in 1656.

> The men received drink rations and special allowances at various stages of the work. First, the men who demolished the old fort received strong beer. When the first stones of the wall were laid the masons were given brandy. Then the carpenters got two barrels of strong beer, three cases of brandy, and small beer when the cellar beams were laid. The men who carried the beams to the carpenters from outside the fort received one-half barrel of beer for each beam they carried (a total of 16½ barrels). . . . Additionally, the carriers, teamsters, carpenters, stonecutters, and masons received a gill of brandy and three pints of beer a day. The alcohol bill alone amounted to almost 6% of the total cost of building this government house.

In the early nineteenth century, drinking continued to be important in the lives of craftsmen. For instance, drinking was often a customary part of the apprentice's initiation into the craft, and the "practice of footing—the payment of whiskey to the shop by every newly hired journeyman on his first day of work—established a ritualized means for new workers to be incorporated into the workplace" (Clawson 1989). Johnson (1978: 57) explains the importance of craft drinking customs in the early nineteenth century:

> [Drinking] was a bond between men who lived, worked and played together. . . . Workmen drank with their employers, in situations that employers controlled. The informal mixing of work and leisure and master and wage earner softened and helped legitimate inequality. At the same time, drunkenness remained within the bounds of what the master considered appropriate. For it was in his house that most routine drinking was done, and it was he who bought the drinks.

Today, drinking continues to be a bond among many craftsmen (LeMasters 1975). For instance, construction workers regard drinking on the job, which is still built into every stage of the construction process, as "fun," a spontaneous "for the hell of it" activity, and "new workers are initiated into this drinking culture and expected to engage in it enthusiastically" (Riemer 1979: 105). According to Riemer, "Drinking is not a rarity on building construction projects. Beer drinking is a common practice for many tradesmen and hard liquor (whiskey and brandy) is consumed occasionally. Not all workers accept drinking on the job, and most contractors, builders, and other management personnel are openly against it, but it is usually tolerated within limits" (1979: 103).

Drinking was also an integral part of the early railroaders' work life, and it continues to play an important role in the lives of many railroaders today (Licht 1983; Mannello and Seaman 1979; Eichler, Goldberg, Kier, and Allen 1988). In the nineteenth century, railway workers, when off duty, were most likely to be found in one of the saloons; consequently, the call boy—a young boy who brought the off-duty railroader his work orders—had to know the favored drinking spots of the men (Holbrook 1947). One anonymous railway worker described the railroaders' drinking culture:

> Inured to danger, [railroaders] instinctively cultivate a disposition of reckless and excitable habits. During their trips, the fever of excitement was kept up by the influence of strong drink; and many a man had gained the reputation of being a swift runner and making impossible time when he was half drunk. . . . [Afterwards] they would congregate in the grogshops and beer saloons to recount over their wonderful adventures on the road. . . . [They] would drink to soothe their grievances and demonstrate mutual support; drink evil and bad luck to some obnoxious and tyrannical official and drink long life and prosperity to themselves. (quoted in Licht 1983: 238)

Brakemen were regarded as being "the worst drunkards, gamblers, and rowdies in a profession that was infamous for drinking, drifting, and disorder" (quoted in Reinhardt 1970: 89). Today, drinking remains deeply embedded within the work world of many railroaders. In a study of seven railroads, Mannello and Seaman (1979) reported that 13 percent of operating employees (e.g., engineers, conductors, brakemen) drank while on duty at least once during 1978.

Drinking on the job was also a common practice among America's first factory workers (Rumbarger 1989) and remains a common practice among some assembly line workers (O'Toole 1974; Janes and Ames 1989). For instance, nineteenth-century coopers spent Saturday, which was a regular work day, "lounging about."

> Early on Saturday the brewery wagon would drive up to the shop. Several of the coopers . . . would call out the window to the driver, "Bring me a Goose Egg," meaning a half-barrel of beer, and there would be a merry time all around. . . . Little groups of jolly fellows would often sit around upturned barrels playing poker, using rivets for chips. . . . Usually the good time continued over into Sunday, so that on the following day [Blue Monday] he usually was not in the best condition to settle down to the regular day's work. (Gutman 1976: 37)

Today, automobile assembly-line workers have a reputation as heavy drinkers (Runcie 1980, 1988; Ames and Janes 1987). Ben Hamper (1991: 56), an assembly-line worker turned journalist, writes about his drinking experiences at a General Motors factory: "Drinking right on the line wasn't something everyone cared for. But plenty did, and the most popular time to go snagging for gusto was the lunch break. As soon as that lunch horn blew, half of the plant put it in gear, sprinting out the door in packs of three or four, each pointed squarely for one of those chilly coolers up at one of the nearby beer emporiums."

The military also has a long-lived reputation for heavy drinking (Staudenmeier 1985; West and Swegan 1956; Bray, Marsden, Rachal, and Peterson 1990). The U.S. Navy used to issue a daily ration of "one gill of grog" to sailors, and no ship would set sail without sufficient supplies of alcohol, lest the captain risk a mutiny (Bryant 1974). More recently, Pursch (1976: 1655) described the drinking customs among navy pilots: "We drink according to the following customs: We drink at happy hours, after a good flight, after a bad flight, and after a near mid-air collision (to calm our nerves). . . . We drink when we get our wings, when we get promoted (wetting down parties), when we get passed over (to alleviate our depression). . . . Thus, we drink from enlistment to retirement and from teenhood to old age."

In 1991, the navy's heavy drinking customs were still evident at the Tailhook Association's annual meeting, when drunken naval pilots were accused of sexually harassing and groping at female officers.

Finally, drinking continues to be a part of the work world of many white-collar occupations. Managerial and professional workers still regard drinking at business lunches, company parties, and work-related conferences as normal behavior (Roman 1982; Shore 1985a, 1985b), and some white-collar workers, such as sales representatives and purchasing agents, continue to be known for their heavy drinking practices (Fillmore 1990). In his autobiography, Pete Hamill (1994: 224) provides readers with penetrating examples of the centrality of the drinking life to newspaper work:

> After they gave me my first Working Press card, I brought my familiar sense of entitlement to the bar of the Page One every morning. Those mornings were free of the limits of time, and I would drink with McMorrow, Grove, Poirer, and others, while fishmongers made deliveries and the day-shift guys showed up for a morning pop before starting at ten. The Page One was the headquarters of the fraternity, a place completely devoid of character except for the men at the bar, a way station for all the whiskey-wounded boomers of the business who passed through on their way from one town's paper to another.

Drinking and work remain part of the contemporary American workplace. The persistence of this relationship is remarkable considering the historical efforts made by temperance reformers to rid the workplace of alcohol. In order to understand how the belief that drinking and work do not mix became institutionalized within the American workplace, let us briefly consider some of the temperance reforms supported by employers and workers.

Temperance at Work

The temperance belief that drinking and work do not mix is a social construct (e.g., Conrad and Schneider 1992). By this, I mean that the belief does not reflect some universal law of work life. Rather, it reflects the practices of a particular group that has successfully imposed its definition of the situation on the rest of society so that the belief becomes taken for granted as the correct way to organize work.

Since the eighteenth century, Americans have experienced a series of temperance movements designed to promote sobriety among workers (Blocker 1989). By "sobriety," temperance reformers have meant more than not drinking. Rather, they have meant adopting a particular lifestyle, which emphasizes hard work, discipline, orderliness, frugality, and responsibility (Levine 1989). This definition of temperance reflects Puritans' ideals of communal life.[2]

Ironically, the term *Puritan* conjures up in many Americans' minds the dour visage of a person opposed to all forms of merrymaking, particularly the consumption of alcohol (Tyrrell 1979). This stereotype has little basis in fact. Rather, the Puritans regarded alcohol as "God's Good Gift" (Mather [1673] 1931). They drank such fermented beverages as beer, wine, and ale at most meals and while at work; however, they believed in moderation and were opposed to the abuse of the gift, particularly intemperate drinking that interfered with one's work (Conroy 1991). Within this context, such Puritan ministers as Increase Mather ([1673] 1931) and Cotton Mather ([1708] 1940) preached against the evils of drinking distilled spirits, claiming that rum and whiskey caused the sin of drunken excess and prevented parishioners from fulfilling their social obligations.

Puritan sentiments about alcohol and work were well ingrained within the colonial world. After the American Revolution, however, many Americans began to associate their new liberty with the freedom to drink and, in the postrevolutionary period, Americans consumed large amounts of distilled spirits (Rorabaugh 1979; Lender and Martin 1987). The older Puritan attitudes then became increas-

[2] In coming to America, the Puritans sought to establish God's ideal community on earth (Erikson 1966; Weber 1905). They believed that salvation was freely given by God and that those who had been selected by God for salvation, the Elect, would prosper in the occupations to which they had been called. Consequently, church members were encouraged to work hard and become successful in their callings in order to demonstrate whether they were predestined for salvation or damnation. In addition, the Elect were obligated to act as the community's stewards by using the fruits of their labor to build a harmonious community. As a whole, church members were admonished to accept their callings without complaint, defer to their betters, the Elect, and put the good and safety of the community above self-interests.

ingly attractive to a youthful America's leaders concerned with creating "virtuous citizens" and to employers disciplining workers in
an industrializing country (Lender and Martin 1987; Staudenmeier
1985).[3] For instance, in 1784, Benjamin Rush, the father of American
psychiatry, wrote the early temperance movement's manifesto, *An
Inquiry into the Effects of Ardent Spirits on the Human Mind and Body*.
In this essay, Rush argued that a disease called "inebriety" caused
by drinking distilled spirits was destroying social order.[4] In order to
restore the social order, he counseled people to abstain from drinking distilled spirits and urged employers to serve workers wholesome beverages such as beer, vinegar, milk, and water. Eventually,
temperance reformers would urge national prohibition upon all
Americans; nevertheless, Rush's ideas were the basis for the early
temperance movement (Conrad and Schneider 1992).[5]

Employers: From Temperance to Prohibition

America's temperance movements have generally tried to impose
sobriety on workers rather than to let the concept evolve from the
bottom up. Indeed, between the 1780s and 1920, employers promoted a variety of temperance reforms that culminated in passage
of the Eighteenth Amendment to the United States Constitution: national prohibition (Staudenmeier 1985). Initially, employers sought
to prohibit workers from drinking distilled spirits at work but allowed the consumption of fermented beverages in the workplace.
By the latter half of the nineteenth century, however, many employers had adopted policies prohibiting workers from drinking all al-

---

[3] Benjamin Rush counseled his fellow Americans, if the country allowed drunkenness, with its attendant social and economic problems, to flourish, the American Revolution would have been fought in vain because the country would soon
be governed by men chosen by intemperate and corrupt voters rather than men
of virtue (Rorabaugh 1979; Lender and Martin 1987).
[4] According to Warner (1994), the concept of alcoholism as a progressive disease
predates Rush. He argues that the concept was originally developed by clergy-
men and other moralists in the early seventeenth century and later found acceptance in the British and American medical communities.
[5] For detailed historical discussions of American temperance movements and
their effects upon work, see Staudenmeier 1985, Lender and Martin 1987, Blocker
1989, and Rumbarger 1989.

coholic beverages, including wine and beer, on the job. In addition, some industries and occupations advocated total abstinence or total temperance for workers, prohibiting them from drinking all alcoholic beverages both on and off the job.[6]

Influential farmers and large landowners were the first employers to experiment with Rush's recommendations to provide workers with wholesome alternatives to distilled spirits (Staudenmeier 1985). In 1787, for example, Dr. George Logan reported to the Philadelphia Society for Promoting Agriculture that his temperance experiment had been successful beyond expectations, yielding a large harvest without any fighting or accidents. In 1789, more than two hundred farmers signed the Litchfield Agreement to "carry on our business without the use of distilled spirits" in order to ensure that the laborers would be able to discharge their responsibilities to the community.

By the 1830s, many employers had implemented policies prohibiting workers from drinking at work. Thousands of employers banned distilled spirits from their fields and shops (Blocker 1989); in 1833, the American Temperance Society estimated that seven hundred vessels sailed as "temperance ships" that did not permit sailors to drink distilled spirits on board (Staudenmeier 1985). Some employers adopted a policy of "total abstinence," refusing to hire workers who drank any alcoholic beverages including beer, wine, and ale. For instance, in 1829, one New York City employer reported that "total abstinence is gaining ground" with "astonishing rapidity" among trades once notorious for their drinking (quoted in Wilentz 1985: 146–47). Likewise, in the 1840s, the Good Intent stage coach line and eight eastern railroads resolved that they would not hire workers "who ever drink intoxicating beverages" (Staudenmeier 1985: 76).

During the latter half of the nineteenth century, saloons became the workingman's club, providing workers with such services as check cashing privileges, space for union meetings, free lunches, and employment information (Rosenzweig 1983; Duis 1983). Employers regarded the saloons as hotbeds of unionization, where the name of Karl Marx was too easily spoken and violent strikes were

---

[6] Total temperance is often referred to as teetotalism; this policy was first advocated by the American Temperance Society in the 1830s (Blocker 1989).

too easily fomented (Blocker 1989). In order to deter workers from drinking, employers implemented a number of antisaloon policies, including industrial betterment programs and campaigns to pass prohibitionist legislation (Rumbarger 1989).

Under the guise of industrial betterment, employers implemented a wide range of activities, including educational programs for workers and their children, libraries, recreational activities, and social halls (Brandes 1970). Although industrial betterment was a general policy for winning the hearts and minds of workers, it was also intended to combat the saloons by providing workers with alternative services and gathering places free from the evils of drink (Rumbarger 1989). Railroads, among the first to adopt industrial betterment policies, developed YMCAs and reading rooms for crew members spending nights away from home in order to provide them with alternatives to the warmth of saloons (Licht 1983; Ducker 1983). Steel mills and mines also adopted industrial betterment as a means of controlling the transient hobo element, workers, usually young and unmarried, who, because of labor scarcity, floated from job to job and were inclined to spend their wages in the saloons (Rumbarger 1989).

In the first half of the nineteenth century, some employers also supported campaigns to pass local legislation prohibiting the manufacture, sale, and consumption of alcohol. For instance, during the 1840s and 1850s, employers were influential in passing such laws in several northeastern and midwestern states (Blocker 1989; Rumbarger 1989). It was the failure of industrial betterment policies, however, to contain the saloons and hobo element that induced employers in 1914 to put their full weight behind the drive that resulted in national prohibition (Blocker 1989; Powers 1991). According to Rumbarger, "What made Rockefeller and others spend money for prohibition was the belief in its ability to end the instability of the nation's industrial labor force as a menace to business prosperity" (1989: 183).

Workers: From Temperance to Prohibition

Although efforts to promote sobriety among workers were generally initiated by employers, some workers, either as individuals or union members, also were involved in promoting temperance at work. Their orientation toward temperance however, was generally different from their employers' orientation (Blocker 1989). Whereas employers saw sobriety as the means to increased productivity, workers saw it as the means to social respectability. By sobriety, workers generally meant moderate drinking; however, they also supported reform programs emphasizing total abstinence for ine- briates. Employers and workers shared a belief that drinking prob- lems were essentially caused by some defect in the individual and that their remedy required individual solutions.

Between 1800 and 1920, workers promoted a number of temper- ance reform programs designed to create self-respect for workers and win them a measure of social respectability within the national community. Within the community of craftsmen, temperance was one response to the emergence of large manufacturing establish- ments and the economic depression of 1837–43 (Tyrrell 1979). Dur- ing this period, many master craftsmen lost their shops and either became unemployed or were forced to work as journeymen or fore- men in the new manufacturing establishments. Before the depres- sion, many crafts had developed beneficial societies to protect themselves from economic hardships; as economic conditions turned harsher, however, many of the societies added a temperance theme to their mutual protection function.[7] This temperance theme blamed the hard economic times on workers' intemperate habits and stressed that their survival meant embracing sobriety and fru- gality. Other workers organized temperance beneficial societies, the most successful of which was the Washington Temperance Society.

The Washington Temperance Society, established in 1840, was dedicated to reforming chronic drunkards whom other groups con- sidered unredeemable (Tyrrell 1979; Blumberg, 1991). The society was organized in Baltimore by six craftsmen: a tailor, a carpenter, a coachmaker, a silversmith, a wheelwright, and a blacksmith. The Washingtonians recruited members with spellbinding stories of their hardships from drinking, their inability to control their desires to drink, and their new-found abstinence, which allowed them to live productive lives and care for their families. The Washingtonian pro-

---

[7] The crafts have always espoused a mutual aid ethic. In the Middle Ages, for ex- ample, the guilds provided their members with a variety of welfare benefits, in- cluding unemployment, health, and burial insurance. Likewise, the early craft unions were organized as beneficial societies providing for the needs of their members (Kranzberg and Gies 1975; Clawson 1989).

gram, which appealed to the craftsmen's ethic of mutual aid, consisted of requiring members to sign a pledge of total abstinence and doing whatever was necessary to help one another maintain sobriety. In addition, the Washingtonians taught that "by saving others, they simultaneously saved themselves." Consequently, members combed the docks, streets, vice districts, and gutters to find drunkards and bring them to meetings.

The Washingtonians quickly became a mass movement, attracting a large working-class and middle-class following, as well as many professional workers (Tyrrell 1979). For instance, Neal Dow, successful businessman and ardent supporter of total abstinence, organized a group of Washingtonians in Portland, Maine, and within one year enrolled fourteen hundred workers (Blocker 1989). By March 1842, in New York City, there were at least thirty-eight Washingtonian organizations, many representing specific trades such as the hatters, the bakers, the carpenters, and the butchers (Tyrrell 1979).

Although the Washingtonians died out in the mid-1840s, they were the model for many subsequent fraternal organizations dedicated to reforming drunkards.[8] Among these were the reform clubs, which, by the 1880s, estimated their membership at several hundred thousand and had become the backbone of the working-class temperance movement (Blocker 1989; Lender and Martin 1987). The most prominent reform clubs of this era were the Blue, Red, and White Ribbon Clubs. The Blue and Red Ribbon Clubs were both developed by reformed drunkards. The White Ribbon Clubs were created by the Woman's Christian Temperance Union, which attempted to spark a moral rebirth in drunken workers by preaching the gospel to them and urging them to join the Red and Blue Ribbon Clubs in order to become sober. Where such groups were lacking, they established their own White Ribbon Clubs.

In the latter half of the nineteenth century, unions often found themselves in conflict over the working-class culture that had taken root in the saloons (Rosenzweig 1983; Duis 1983). Although union leaders recognized the value of the services the saloons provided their members, some organizations such as the National Labor Union, the Knights of Labor, the National Colored Labor Union, the

---

[8] The Washingtonians were also a prototype for the first asylums for the treatment of inebriates (Baumohl and Room 1987).

Amalgamated Association of Iron and Steel Workers, and the Brotherhood of Locomotive Engineers saw the saloons as undermining the labor movement (Staudenmeier 1985; Blocker 1989). As early as the 1830s, for example, the General Trade Union of New York City "promoted a code of radical rectitude that would have taken their men out of the taverns, cockpits and brothels and into committee rooms and lecture halls to combat their common enemies" (Wilentz 1985: 255). Similarly, in the 1880s and 1890s, some union leaders condemned saloonkeepers as social parasites who enslaved workers for the corporation, and they urged their members to adopt a sober lifestyle committed to building a strong labor movement. As one railway man put it, "As soon as a man has spent all his money for drink he becomes a slave of the corporation" (quoted in Blocker 1989: 69).

In addition to being the locus of the working-class culture, saloons were also the centers of political corruption (Rosenzweig 1983; Duis 1983). Political bosses often used the saloons as their headquarters and employed regular patrons to stuff the ballot boxes and to terrorize their opponents. By 1910, these activities had firmly convinced most labor leaders that the saloons had become a menace to the working class. This belief was well exemplified by a 1907 San Francisco scandal, which revealed that the saloon-based political machine behind the Union Labor party was more interested in pursuing government graft and bribes from businessmen than in pursuing the long-term welfare of its working-class constituents (Powers 1991). As a result, workers attending union meetings heard many disturbing arguments for breaking off their long-term relationship with the saloon. According to Powers, "Barroom regulars might scoff at antisaloon tirades of pious middle-class reformers, but the hardheaded arguments of labor advocates could not be as easily dismissed. Even then most workers were not prepared to reject the saloon simply on the advice of unions, but neither, perhaps, were they prepared to defend it when the final showdown came in 1920" (1991: 122).

National Prohibition: The Short-Lived Experiment

The Eighteenth Amendment was never very popular with most Americans, who preferred either its repeal or its replacement with legislative controls on alcohol sales in order to promote moderate consumption (Engelmann 1979; Kyvig 1979). Nevertheless, despite the enduring images of bootleg liquor, gangsters, and G-men, most Americans complied with the law, which reduced alcohol consumption and alcohol-related deaths (Lender and Martin 1987; Levine and Reinarman 1993).

Likewise in the workplace, the majority of workers complied with national prohibition because most had quit drinking on the job before its enactment (Gusfield 1991). Prohibition, however, did not deter workers in some occupations from continuing to drink at work. One railroader recounted how bootleggers replaced the saloons in the railroad town where he grew up and how the shortage of workers forced the railroad to hire and protect drinkers even though drinking was against company policy and national law:

> The railroad yard was the favorite gathering place of the town's sporting element. . . . The boomers got in the habit of doing their drinking at the yard. They would line up against the edge of the freighthouse platform, with a half-gallon fruit jar for a wassail bowl, while the police hid in the adjoining lumber yard, hoping one of the celebrators would get drunk enough to stagger out of the neutral zone, whereupon he could be seized and dragged into court. (quoted in Reinhardt 1970: 165–66)

In 1933, the Eighteenth Amendment was repealed because most Americans, including management and labor, had become convinced that rather than uniting the country, national prohibition was tearing it apart (Kyvig 1979). Within the corporate community, the drive for repeal was led by the Association Against the Prohibition Amendment (AAPA), which feared a federal government so strong that it could wipe out an entire industry at the stroke of a pen and so weak that it could not enforce the laws on the books. As John Raskob, a General Motors executive and AAPA supporter, said, "If the Prohibition Amendment and laws at present on its books . . . are resulting in a lack of respect for law, it is but a short step to such lack of respect for property rights as to result in bolshevism" (Kyvig 1979: 84). Similarly, the American Federation of Labor pressed for repeal, arguing that Prohibition "had failed in its avowed purpose and was largely responsible for the present economic conditions [i.e., the depression]" (quoted in Engelmann 1979: 188). In 1929, President

Hoover's National Commission on Law Observance and Enforcement concluded that Prohibition, rather than domesticating workers, had produced a resentful working class, which believed that the law was applied unfairly to workers, who could not obtain decent beer and wine for their household tables while the wealthy could purchase all the liquor they wanted (Rumbarger 1989).[9] Consequently, as the depression deepened, businessmen and workers united behind the AAPA, arguing that repeal would produce economic prosperity (Kyvig 1979). President Roosevelt signed legislation repealing Prohibition on December 5, 1933.

Employee Assistance Programs

Since the repeal of the Eighteenth Amendment in 1933, labor and management have continued to encourage sobriety among workers. As in earlier times, intemperance has been seen as a problem of the individual. Since the creation of Alcoholics Anonymous (AA) in 1935, however, problem drinkers have increasingly been defined as suffering from a treatable illness called "alcoholism"[10] (Conrad and Schneider 1992), and labor and management have generally sought to treat rather than punish alcoholic workers (Trice and Beyer 1984).[11] Today, the principal means of treating alcoholic workers are employee assistance programs (Blum and Roman 1989).

Employee assistance programs are rooted in the traditions of AA, which, like the Washingtonians and the reform clubs before them, promotes sobriety by encouraging recovering alcoholics to help other alcoholics (Trice and Schonbrunn 1981; Roman 1981). Em-

[9] There was much truth to this claim (Lender and Martin 1987; Blocker 1989). Illegal alcohol was expensive, and bootleggers tended to produce more hard liquor than beer or wine because it was more lucrative and portable. Consequently, lower-class drinkers, who generally preferred beer anyway, consumed less alcohol because they could not afford the inflated prices of bootleg liquor. Affluent middle- and upper-class drinkers, who generally preferred hard liquors and could afford the inflated prices, continued to consume alcohol at close to their old rates of consumption.

[10] In contrast to Rush's concept of inebriety, which posits that the disease is caused by alcohol's effects upon the body, AA posits that alcoholism is caused by defects within the individual (Alcoholics Anonymous 1955).

[11] For a detailed discussion, see Sonnenstuhl 1986.

ployee assistance programs identify alcoholic employees, motivate them to accept help for their drinking problems, and refer them to community-based organizations such as AA and in-patient treatment for help (Trice and Roman 1972). They also define alcohol problems within the framework of industrial jurisprudence, which is designed to protect workers from being unfairly disciplined (Denenberg and Denenberg 1991). Within this framework, alcohol problems are defined as drinking that interferes with an employee's job performance, and the suspected alcoholic is motivated to accept help by use of a combination of progressive discipline and offers of help, a strategy called "constructive confrontation" (Trice and Roman 1972).[12]

Employee assistance programs have been relatively successful at helping alcoholic employees to gain sobriety, typically reporting recovery rates of 70 percent or better (e.g., Trice and Beyer 1984; Walsh et al. 1991; Blum and Roman 1989). Nevertheless, as the Woodlawn subway disaster illustrates, employee assistance programs, like earlier temperance efforts, have had limited success at deterring on-the-job drinking in some occupations because co-workers, following an occupational norm of cover-up, protect the drinkers.[13] In the railroad industry, for instance, Mannello and Seaman (1979; see also Hitchcock and Sanders 1976) found that, despite the treatment success of its programs, 13 percent of the operating personnel drank at least once while on duty during 1978 and that their co-workers failed to do anything to prevent it. In their study of a manufacturing plant, Ames and her colleagues (Ames, Delaney, and Janes 1992; De-

[12] This strategy requires a supervisor to confront the suspected employee with evidence of unsatisfactory performance and to coach him or her on how to improve his or her work, while simultaneously emphasizing the consequences of continued poor performance. If the employee's performance does not improve after several informal discussions, the supervisor implements standard, formal disciplinary procedures, beginning with spoken warnings and progressing through written notices, suspension and discharge. At each of these steps, the employee is urged to seek help from the employee assistance program for any personal problems which may be adversely affecting his or her performance.
[13] Labor has been ambivalent about employee assistance programs (Trice and Roman 1972; Roman 1981). On one hand, labor leaders want the treatment benefits for their members; on the other hand, they fear that management may use the program as a smoke screen for firing union members. Despite its misgivings, labor has been supportive of employee assistance programs that safeguard workers' jobs (AFL-CIO 1993; Trice, Hunt, and Beyer 1981; Jacobs and Zimmer 1991).

laney and Ames 1993) found that union stewards, believing that their primary responsibility was to protect co-workers from management complaints, threatened to file a grievance whenever supervisors tried to refer workers to the employee assistance program. As a result, workers felt that they could drink on the job if they chose and that it was unlikely that drinking would result in disciplinary action.[14]

Like earlier workplace temperance efforts, today's employee assistance programs have failed to prevent on-the-job drinking within some occupations. As the railroad and assembly-line studies discussed earlier suggest, this failure is due to the temperance movements' focus upon reforming individual drinkers rather than upon changing the workplace. As Straus (1975) observed, workplace alcohol programs are "aimed at detection and rehabilitation or at modifying the drinker's behavior through education. . . . They do not address the more basic question of identifying what it is about work situations and work experiences that makes it meaningful for employees to drink too much or what preventive intervention might modify these conditions."

The Need to Transform Occupational Cultures

In this book, I argue that, in order for sobriety to develop within those occupations that have been resistant to previous temperance efforts, the workers' intemperate occupational drinking culture must be transformed. By "occupational drinking culture," I mean workers who share a common identity of themselves as a distinctive category of workers and distinctive beliefs about drinking. Some occupations, such as accountants and university professors, for example, possess temperate drinking cultures that generally discourage heavy consumption of alcoholic beverages and confine drinking among occupational members to leisure time (Andrews, Watkins, and Cosper 1983). In contrast, some occupations, such as railroaders, auto assembly-line workers, construction workers, naval officers, and sales representatives, support intemperate drinking

---

[14] In a companion piece, Ames and Delaney (1992) document how supervisors also collaborate in covering up for workers.

cultures that encourage heavy consumption of alcoholic beverages and permit members to drink together both on and off the job, melding work and leisure.

Members of intemperate occupational drinking cultures do not perceive on-the-job drinking as deviant behavior (e.g., Cosper 1979). Rather, within intemperate drinking cultures, on-the-job drinking is regarded as normal behavior and experienced as a ritual, a stereotyped set of behaviors that creates feelings of solidarity and bonds occupational members into a community of equals, distinguishing them from other workers (Durkheim 1912/1954; Turner 1969; Collins 1988). Because rituals are emotionally rewarding, members experience on-the-job drinking as occupational conformity rather than deviance. In order for intemperate drinking cultures to be transformed into temperate drinking cultures, some occupational members must redefine drinking as deviance rather than conformity, teach these new meanings to other members, and create new rituals for reconstructing feelings of solidarity.

Although culture has become a major focus for the study and management of modern organizations (Gamst 1989; Martin 1992; Frost et al. 1991; Trice and Beyer 1993), there has been no consideration of how unions characterized by intemperate occupational drinking cultures can transform those cultures into ones of sobriety. By focusing on one union's efforts to transform its intemperate occupational drinking culture I hope to reveal what makes intemperate drinking meaningful to workers and the social processes involved in transforming such deeply embedded rituals. In this book I examine the drinking culture of the Tunnel and Construction Workers Union,[15] a craft union of hard rock miners in New York City who are known as the "sandhogs," and how, after drinking intemperately for nearly a hundred years, they are transforming their intemperate drinking culture into a temperate drinking one.

Some occupations have intemperate occupational drinking cultures that have been highly resistant to temperance reformers' efforts to create a sober workforce. In Chapter 2, I present a framework for understanding why some workers perpetuate intemperate

---

[15] Officially, the union is the Compressed Air and Free Air, Shaft, Tunnel, Foundation, Caisson, Subway, Cofferdam, Sewer Construction Workers of New York & New Jersey States & Vicinity, Local 147, Laborers' International Union, AFL-CIO.

occupational drinking cultures and how they can transform them into temperate ones. Essentially, intemperate drinking is a ritual that marks the occupation's boundary and creates a sense of solidarity among members, and intemperate drinking cultures will not be transformed until drinking loses its ritual effect within the occupation. This occurs when some occupational members challenge the group's intemperate drinking norms, introduce alternative norms of sobriety, and are able to mobilize the resources to make their definition of the situation the dominant one.

In Chapters 3, 4, and 5, I apply the framework presented in Chapter 2 to the case of the sandhogs. In Chapter 3, I describe the development of the sandhogs as a tightly knit occupational community. In Chapter 4, I describe how their drinking rituals mark their communal boundary and create a sense of solidarity among members. In Chapter 5, I describe how the sandhogs are transforming their intemperate culture into one of sobriety by helping one another remain sober and challenging the belief that one must drink in order to be a sandhog. In Chapter 6, I summarize my theoretical argument and discuss its generalizability to the transformation of other intemperate drinking cultures.

2 Understanding the Persistence and Transformation of Intemperate Drinking Cultures

*A*lthough temperance reformers have been successful in removing drink from most American work organizations, some workers continue to build their communal lives around drinking alcohol. From the outside, this behavior appears highly irrational to most Americans, who now take it for granted that work and alcohol do not mix. This chapter presents an alternative framework for understanding the persistence of intemperate drinking behavior and its transformation. I argue that, when viewed from inside the occupational community, intemperate drinking is a ritual that permits members to continuously reconstruct their culture and solidify their communal bonds and that these practices will not change until drinking loses its symbolic hold over community members.

Occupational Culture and Community Defined

Culture has many definitions in the social sciences; however, its most basic definition is that of shared meanings that guide social action (Alexander and Seidman 1990).[1] Swindler (1986) provides a useful definition of culture as a tool kit of symbols, stories, rituals, and

[1] As culture has become a growing area of research for both sociologists and organizational theorists, there has been much debate over how the shared meanings

world views for solving the problems of living. From this tool kit, actors construct strategies of action for solving their problems of living. Strategies of action consist of the group's basic assumptions about the nature of its problems of living, beliefs about the appropriate ways of solving those problems, and cultural forms such as stories, rituals, and social accounts that communicate those basic assumptions and beliefs to the group's members. In contrast to individual lines of action, which are constructed within individual definitions of a situation (e.g., Blumer 1969; Charon 1992), strategies of action are a group phenomenon, and they are persistent ways of ordering action through time. In relatively stable periods, actors take the previously constructed strategies of action for granted, regarding them as either traditional practices or common sense; however, during periods of social transformation, actors construct from their tool kit new ideologies, which are highly articulated, self-conscious belief and ritual systems offering a unified answer to social action.

Within Swindler's framework, an occupational culture may be understood as a strategy of action for gaining jurisdiction over a set of tasks within the labor market, and an occupation is a group of workers whose beliefs have become institutionalized within the labor market. By institutionalized, I mean that the group's beliefs about the tasks composing its work are recognized within the labor market as the legitimate way to organize such tasks and, as a result of that perception, the group's members, who are seen as possessing special knowledge, are given jurisdiction over the performance of those tasks (Hughes 1958; Freidson 1982; Abbott 1988).[2] In turn, because the group has jurisdiction over those tasks, work organiza-

---

called "culture" guide peoples' actions. For instance, structural-functionalists present culture as a highly stable entity that provides actors a complete blueprint for living and the actors as constrained to the blueprint's line of action (e.g., Parsons 1937, 1951). In contrast, symbolic interactionists present culture as a relatively fluid environment from which actors construct their own lines of action (e.g., Hewitt 1989). For useful overviews and critiques of the different perspectives on culture in sociology and organizational theory, see Crane 1994 and Martin 1992.

[2] State licensure is one mechanism by which a group's beliefs are recognized as the legitimate way of organizing work. Thus, within the latter half of the nineteenth century, a wide range of occupations including barbers, plumbers, blacksmiths, doctors, and pharmacists requested licensure from the state as a means of controlling their labor markets. Today, developing occupations continue to seek licensure as a means of controlling their markets. In providing licensure, the states have accepted the occupations' standards for what are minimal requirements for a person to perform their particular tasks (Trice 1993).

tions, in order to maintain their own legitimacy, are compelled to hire only members of the group to perform those tasks (Meyer and Rowan 1977; DiMaggio and Powell 1983). These institutionalization patterns emerge through a historical process. While appearing at any point in time as unique to the present work situation, these patterns, even the most informal, can be traced to the historical construction and transformation of an occupational culture.

An occupational culture becomes institutionalized as a group of workers struggles to gain and maintain a monopoly over the performance of their work (Freidson 1982; Abbott 1988). Workers begin constructing an occupational culture when they are brought together to perform particular tasks (Salaman 1986). In order to make sense of their shared work experiences, they make basic assumptions about their relationship to one another and their work environment, and these beliefs become the basis of stories they tell one another and of rituals they construct to create a sense of communal solidarity among themselves (Trice 1993). These stories and rituals highlight what the workers need to know to perform their work, the skills and techniques of the job, as well as the appropriate ways to relate to the boss and one's co-workers. In addition, the stories and rituals underscore for workers their common stake in their work and their differences from other kinds of workers; they are the raw materials from which the workers construct an occupational identity—an image of themselves as possessing special knowledge, skills, and qualities.

Stories and rituals are also the basis for socializing new occupational members (Trice 1993). By listening to the stories and participating in the rituals, newcomers learn that people like those in the group act this way and, in order for newcomers to be regarded as occupational members, they must act this way too. In this manner, newcomers also learn the social accounts that occupational members use to justify their actions to themselves and outsiders. Initially, such training may occur informally on the job. Later, as the workers gain some control over their work and the recruitment of newcomers, the training may occur in formal apprenticeship programs or even in universities.

Occupational stories are also the basis for workers' claims to employers, other workers, clients, legislators, and government agencies that their group ought to have jurisdiction over the performance of their tasks and that nonmembers ought to be excluded from performing such work. In these instances, the stories function as accounts or justifications to these other groups, emphasizing the workers' special knowledge and unique capacities for performing their work. Other groups may either reject or accept the workers' justifications for excluding nonmembers and either grant or deny the group of workers a monopoly over their claimed work. Acceptance and the granting of jurisdiction by other groups indicate that the workers' beliefs, as communicated through their stories, have become institutionalized within the labor market; that is, the group of workers has been recognized as an occupation.

Consequently, the boundary the occupation struggles to draw around its work in order to exclude nonmembers is symbolically constructed (Cohen 1985), based upon the stories which they tell one another and the rituals they use to include those individuals who know the appropriate ways to act. The struggle to construct and maintain an occupational boundary creates in members a sense of community, a consciousness of the beliefs, stories, rituals, and social accounts that they hold in common and which distinguish them from other workers (Gusfield 1975; Van Maanen and Barley 1984; Cohen 1985). The shared beliefs, stories, rituals, and social accounts resulting from shared work experiences constitute the workers' occupational culture, and they are the basis for insiders' recognition of one another and exclusion of outsiders. This consciousness of kind, which always develops in conjunction with a consciousness of differences (Weber [1922] 1968), constitutes the basic communal bond that holds the occupational community together and marks its boundary. An occupational community, then, is a group of workers bound together by a common work culture. Whereas *occupation* denotes formal recognition by others of the members' beliefs, *occupational community* denotes members' recognition of one another based upon their common culture.

Culture is a mechanism for ensuring an occupational community's survival (Trice 1993); thus, an occupational culture is formally defined as a pattern of basic assumptions—invented, discovered, or developed by a group of workers as it learns to cope with its problems of external adaptation and internal integration—that has worked well enough to be considered valid and, therefore, to be taught to new members as the correct way to perceive, think, and feel in relation to those problems (Schein 1985: 9). Workers, as they struggle to make sense of their world, develop deeply held beliefs about their relationships with one another and their work environment. These beliefs guide members in constructing their relationships with one another and outsiders and are passed on to new generations in the form of occupational stories and rituals. They are accepted truths about the way the group's work ought to be organized and, therefore, are experienced by members as morally compelling. The formation of an occupational culture, then, parallels occupational formation because the essence of group identity or consciousness of kind is the shared pattern of beliefs that result from shared work experiences.

Workers are guided in the construction of their occupational communities by their basic cultural assumptions (Sonnenstuhl and Trice 1991). Some workers, for example, perceive their relationships with management and the rest of the world as being adversarial, and they construct tightly bounded occupational communities. They assume that the world is extremely dangerous and that their survival depends upon maintaining a tightly knit group whose members face adversity together. These assumptions give rise to a community whose culture puts primary emphasis upon preserving the group by drawing a rigid boundary around its work and subjugating communal members to its collective will. In addition, these assumptions lead to the creation of an occupational community in which members experience strong communal bonds with one another. Members of occupational communities build their sense of self around their work role, take members of the occupational community as their primary reference group, and, preferring to spend time with their own kind, integrate their work and leisure activities (e.g., Salaman 1974; Van Maanen and Barley 1984; Trice 1993).[3]

Rituals are a primary mechanism by which a group conveys its basic assumptions to members and creates communal bonds among them (e.g., Durkheim [1912] 1954; Turner 1969; Alexander

[3] According to Salaman (1974), workers who are highly involved in their work are likely to develop tightly knit occupational communities. Several factors lead workers to become highly involved in their work and consequently develop strong communal bonds: (1) skilled work that requires special knowledge and skills, (2) work that is relatively free of supervision, (3) work that takes place under extreme conditions, makes unusual emotional demands upon workers, or both, and (4) work that is defined as fulfilling important social functions.

1990).[4] Collins (1988) provides a useful way to conceptualize any ritual, whether it is a large-scale ceremony, such as a wedding or school graduation, or a small-scale interaction ritual, such as a greeting or an act of superior-subordinate deference. He argues that all rituals, whether they occur spontaneously in the course of everyday interactions or are initiated intentionally, have the following elements in common: (1) the assembly of a group, (2) a common focus of attention and the group's mutual awareness of that common focus, (3) a common emotional mood that is shared by the group, and (4) a sacred object or symbol that is representative of membership in the group. According to Collins, "participation in rituals gives individuals a new fund of emotional energy" (1988: 195). This fund of emotional energy is rewarding to those who participate in the rituals, and they want to continue to participate in future group rituals. Thus, by producing emotionally rewarding experiences, rituals also reconfirm an individual's identity with the group and encourage individual compliance with group expectations for appropriate behavior (MacKinnon 1994).

Some work processes are emotionally engaging; Collins refers to these as naturally occurring rituals because, as workers interact with one another, the interaction naturally produces ritual effects. The work processes are experienced by workers as emotionally engaging or rewarding because the work processes have all of the ritual elements embedded within them (Collins 1988). As workers interact with one another, they naturally experience renewed bursts of energy that strengthen their communal bonds.[5]

[4] Ritual has a variety of meanings within the social sciences (e.g., Douglas 1970; Goffman 1974, Geertz 1973; Trice and Beyer 1993; Lukes 1975; Kunda 1992). Although social scientists may vehemently disagree about how to define ritual, "most would agree that in both its social and psychological consequences, ritual confirms and strengthens social identity and people's sense of social location: It is an important means through which people experience community" (Cohen 1985: 50).

[5] According to Collins the ritual elements in naturally occurring work rituals are variables, and the degree of communal bonding (i.e., the ritual effects) produced by the work processes is directly related to the strength of those variables. For instance, workers who experience ritual effects work in a group, and the larger the group the larger the ritual effects. Second, within the work group, members have a common work focus of which they are mutually aware—performing the group tasks—and the more that group members exercise control over their tasks, the greater will be their focus, mutual awareness, and the ritual effects produced. Third, work group members who experience ritual effects also share a common

The work of coal mining, for instance, is characterized by all of the elements of ritual and naturally produces ritual effects as miners interact on the job with one another (Fitzpatrick 1980). Coal miners work in crews under very dangerous circumstances that focus their attention on their common tasks and common mood, and as the crew members interact with one another, they use a distinctive language, which symbolizes their communal life, to accomplish their tasks and alert one another to possible dangers. This interaction naturally strengthens crew members' identity with, and commitment to, their mining community and its members.

Communal bonds are also strengthened when members intentionally enact such occupational rituals as initiation, graduation, and degradation ceremonies (e.g., McCarl 1984; Trice 1993). For instance, coal miners engage in a number of sexually explicit initiation games, including "paddling," "dusting," and "pretty pecker" contests, which have the function of "subordinat[ing] the will of the individual to the group" (Vaught and Smith 1980: 164). Although such activities may be viewed as perverse when abstracted from the work of coal mining, they are powerful rituals, when intentionally enacted, further strengthening miners' communal bonds by reconfirming what it means to be a miner and underscoring one's obligations to the work group.

Persistence of Intemperate Occupational Drinking

Intemperate occupational drinking persists because the consumption of alcohol is an intentionally enacted ritual, which reinforces an occupational community's basic assumptions and strengthens members' communal bonds. Intemperate drinking is always a group activity practiced within the context of the occupational community's ongoing relations. In these group settings, members of the occupational community share a common focus (i.e., drinking and

---

emotional mood, such as the experience of coping with dangerous working conditions, and the stronger the emotional mood shared by workers, the stronger the ritual effects. Fourth, group membership is symbolically represented by the special argot members must use to communicate with one another and by the special tools they use to perform their work.

other work-related activities) and common emotional moods (e.g., playfulness, pride of craftsmanship, a sense of danger), and alcohol consumption acts as a symbol of members' communal life. Consequently, intemperate occupational drinking triggers ritual effects: members of the occupational community experience a heightened sense of energy and identification with their occupational community. At the same time, occupational drinking also reinforces beliefs about outsiders and the obligations and duties community members owe to one another. This occurs because one drinks with one's own kind and excludes nonmembers from occupational drinking.

Longshoremen, for example, possess an elaborate drinking culture that defines one's status within the occupational community (Mars 1987). In Newfoundland, the longshoremen are organized into two groups, the regulars who are consistently rehired on the work gangs and the outside men who are erratically employed on the gangs. Regulars drink beer with other regulars in tavern settings and recognize an obligation to recruit one another on their work gangs. Outside men drink wine or rum with other outside men; however, because they do not have regular employment, outside men confine their drinking with other longshoremen to the docks. Drinking marks this occupational community's boundaries, as well as its internal stratification system, by creating a consciousness of kind. According to Mars,

> Drinking is so important to nearly all longshoremen that it is common to find it used as a basis of assessments. Men are judged as men by how well they carry their drink and by how generously they spend their money on drink. There is correspondingly strong suspicion of the small minority of men who do not drink. When early in fieldwork, I asked a group of longshoremen why someone who was married, young, fit and hard-working—all well regarded qualities in a workmate—was nonetheless an outside man, the answer given was that he was a "loner." When I queried what form this took, I was told, "He doesn't drink—that's what I mean by a loner." (1987: 91)

Intemperate occupational drinking must also be understood as a ritual of resistance (Lurie 1979; Braithwaite 1989), as a symbol of workers' revolt against employers' attempts to impose discipline upon workers. According to Johnson (1978: 60), in the 1820s, as employment shifted from household workshops to small factories, drinking that had been "an ancient bond between classes had become, within a very short time, an angry badge of working-class status." Today, intemperate drinking continues to be an angry badge of working-class status in such occupational communities as mining (Gouldner 1954), assembly-line work (Ames and Janes 1987), and construction (Riemer 1979). For instance, it has been a way of life on the railroads since the nineteenth century, and management has been unable to stamp it out because "the severity of punishment [against railroaders' drinking] created an `us against them' attitude between labor and management" (Eichler et al. 1988: 3).

As a ritual of resistance, intemperate drinking persists in occupational communities where employers have been unable to exert complete control over workers.[6] Within such occupational communities as railroading and construction, workers, often working in teams, continue to exercise a great deal of discretion over their work (Riemer 1979; Eichler et al. 1988).[7] For instance, mine managers have been unable to stamp out intemperate drinking because miners continue to exercise a great deal of control over their work (Goodman and Atkin 1984). Within this context, Gouldner (1954) found that mine managers, faced with the miners' resistance, recognized that the miners were a cohesive group of "tough birds" who could not be "pushed around" and consequently felt that, in order to keep the mines operating, they had little choice but to accept their intemperate drinking as normal behavior.

Occupational communities that retain intemperate drinking rituals also appear to justify them on the basis of the emotional de-

[6] Some studies suggest that alcohol problems are highest among those workers who are not closely supervised because such working conditions provide workers, especially those predisposed to alcohol problems, opportunities to drink (Roman and Trice 1970; Trice and Roman 1972; Roman 1981; Mannello and Seaman 1979). For instance, Trice (1965a, 1965b) in a study of utility workers found that workers employed in such mobile jobs as meter reading were more likely than those in nonmobile jobs to be heavy drinkers and diagnosed as having alcohol problems.

[7] Fillmore (1990) conducted an exploratory study of the relationships between workers developing an intemperate drinking culture, availability of alcohol, and the consumption of alcohol. She concluded that intemperate drinking cultures were most likely to develop in jobs where employees worked in teams and that occupational norms mediate between the sheer availability of alcohol and its consumption.

mands that the work makes upon members.[8] Miners claim that their dangerous working conditions entitle them to special privileges such as heavy drinking (Gouldner 1954); railroaders justify intemperate drinking as a means of coping with the loneliness of being away from home (Eichler et al. 1988); and assembly-line workers justify drinking as a way of coping with the boredom and monotony (Ames and Janes 1987).

Intemperate drinking practices are passed on from one generation of workers to the next so that drinking on the job becomes a taken-for-granted fact of work life (e.g., Zucker 1991). For instance, Riemer describes how old timers initiated new construction workers into the drinking culture: "Jokes and ridicule are often used by the established workers to encourage the initiate. It is not uncommon to hear, `If you're going to be an electrician, then you're going to have to drink like an electrician' " (1979: 105). Initiates also learn the occupational community's justifications for drinking.

Intemperate occupational drinking persists because, as a ritual passed on from generation to generation, alcohol consumption is emotionally engaging and enhances bonding among community members. As a result, members take it for granted that drinking is a natural part of their work role and incorporate drinking into their communal sense of self. Intemperate occupational drinking, then, is a ritual that conveys to and reinforces among members the community's basic assumptions. At the same time, intemperate drinking behavior marks the occupational community's boundary by distinguishing insiders from outsiders. If drinking is such an integral part of an occupational community's culture and so deeply embedded within its communal life, how are such practices transformed?

Transforming Intemperate Drinking

Although change agents speak dramatically of changing cultures (e.g., Deal and Kennedy 1982), most often they are concerned about trans-

---

[8] A number of studies report positive correlations between stressful working conditions, escapist reasons for drinking, and alcohol consumption, and their findings suggest that cultural prescriptions mediate between stressful conditions and alcohol consumption (Fennell, Rodin, and Kantor 1981; Harris and Fennell 1988; Martin, Blum, and Roman 1992).

forming specific aspects of an organization's culture rather than changing its entire culture (Schein 1985; Trice and Beyer 1993). Indeed, it is rarely possible to change basic assumptions because they are so deeply embedded within the organization's everyday life. But it is not necessarily desirable to change such deep meanings when agents are attempting to change such specific behaviors as intemperate drinking, because some aspects of the existing culture may not be in conflict with the new behavior and may be used to support the new behavior.

Generally, because culture is a mechanism for ensuring an occupational community's survival, change may be precipitated by disruptions either within its environment or in members' relationships to one another (Schein 1985; Wuthnow 1987). Such disruptions disturb the presumptions surrounding members' actions, temporarily allowing members to question their behavior and construct new shared meanings for their new circumstances. Members may experiment with new beliefs in order to make sense of their new circumstances. If the new beliefs work, they may replace the old ones. But if they do not work or do not work any better than the old beliefs, the old ones may be maintained.

The transformation of intemperate drinking rituals requires a conscious effort to construct a new definition of drinking within the occupational community and the mobilization of resources to teach members that new meaning and to sustain it until the old rituals fade and the new meaning replaces it. That is, the belief that one does not have to drink to be a member of the occupational community becomes a social fact. According to Swindler, "In unsettled periods, differences in ritual practices or doctrine may become highly charged. . . . Ritual acquires such significance in unsettled lives because ritual changes reorganize taken-for-granted habits and modes of experience. People developing new strategies of action depend on cultural models to learn styles of self, relationship, cooperation, authority, and so forth" (1986: 279).

The transformation of intemperate drinking cultures occurs in a three-stage occupational rite of passage (Van Gennep [1908] 1960). As for other rites of passage, the three stages are unfreezing, transformation, refreezing.[9] The occupational community is transformed

[9] Van Gennep ([1908] 1960) suggested that cultural change generally follows a three-stage process which he referred to as "rites of passage": rite of separation, rite of transition, rite of incorporation. This conceptual framework has been adopted

so that its members come to see themselves as being different from the way they were in the past. In the case of intemperate drinking, the occupational community adopts a new set of beliefs about the consumption of alcohol, and its members come to see themselves as temperate.

Unfreezing

In the unfreezing stage, the occupational community's economic environment is disrupted, temporarily calling into question members' accepted beliefs about the efficacy of intemperate drinking rituals as a survival mechanism. In Chapter 1, for example, we saw that the adoption of temperate drinking behavior by Americans was often precipitated by changing political and economic conditions. Washingtonianism was primarily a working-class social movement that evolved partly in reaction to the economic depression of 1837 and partly in reaction to the coercive prohibitionist policies of the American Temperance Society. These changes prompted many workers to question their beliefs about alcohol, and many embraced the Washingtonian movement and its beliefs about abstinence as a mechanism for developing respectability within an emergent industrial society increasingly demanding that workers be temperate in all things. Still, many workers, as well as the occupational communities to which they belonged, did not adopt the Washingtonians' beliefs within their own work lives. Much the same can also be said of workers' reactions to later temperance programs such as the reform clubs and Alcoholics Anonymous.

Leadership is essential for unfreezing intemperate drinking cultures and preparing members of the occupational community for the transformation stage (Schein 1985; Trice and Beyer 1993; McAdam, McCarthy, and Zald 1988). Before change can occur an indigenous leader must arise within the occupational community, take advantage of the disruption, and mobilize the change effort. The Washingtonians grew rapidly because craftsmen such as John Hawkins and Lewis Levin traveled extensively telling their own dramatic recovery stories and encouraging other workers to join the movement as a

---

by other social scientists (e.g., Turner 1969; Moore and Myerhoff 1977; Trice and Beyer 1993), and it is also the basis for Lewin's (1947) well-known schema for creating planned organizational change: unfreezing, change, refreezing.

means "to preserve or to restore their precarious status of respectable artisans" (Tyrrell 1979: 171).

Effective leadership at this stage requires several crucial characteristics. First, the leader must possess a sense of calling in order to summon the courage to go against his community's beliefs (Weber [1905] 1958, [1919] 1958a, [1919] 1958b; Goldman 1988). The leader feels a sense of mission that transcends the constraints of the occupational community and believes that his or her well-being is dependent on fulfilling this mission. This sense of mission was evident in both the leadership and membership of the Washingtonians because they believed that their individual sobriety and livelihood depended upon helping others to remain sober; the same is true of Alcoholics Anonymous (Maxwell 1950, Blumberg 1991). Indeed, it is this sense of mission that drove AA members to work with industrial physicians to develop industrial alcoholism programs during the 1930s, 1940s, and 1950s (Trice and Schonbrunn 1981).

Effective leaders must be able to reframe the occupational community's current beliefs within the framework of the new temperance language. Snow and his colleagues (1986: 464) refer to this process as frame alignment: "the linkage of individual and SMO [Social Movement Organizations] interpretative orientations, such that some set of individual interests, values, and beliefs and SMO activities, goals and ideologies are congruent and complementary." The occupational leader must bring the community's beliefs about drinking into alignment with the new temperance beliefs. This kind of frame alignment occurred in the early labor movement when some labor leaders picked up the Washingtonian belief about helping others to remain sober and connected it with labor's belief in providing members with mutual aid. According to Blocker,

> As trade unions revived with prosperity many workers found them a better weapon than the temperance movement to combat poverty and exploitation. Such workers took with them organizational and oratorical skills learned in the Washingtonian societies and, as well, their appreciation for temperance; this explains why some of the new unions adopted a rule of total abstinence. (1989: 47)

Transformation

Successful social change proceeds from a significant transformation in the collective consciousness of actors (Gamson, Fireman, and Rytina 1982). In the transformation stage, the intemperate drinking culture is changed as the leader recruits new adherents within the occupational community to the new temperance beliefs. According to resource mobilization research, unions provide excellent settings for recruiting new members to social movements because they contain "established structures of solidarity on which most social behavior depends" (McAdam, McCarthy, and Zald 1988: 710). Because individuals value their identity as union members, they do not want to do anything to jeopardize their involvement in the community; the most effective social movement organization recruitment appeals within unions are framed in a manner that taps recruits' commitment to this salient identity (e.g., McAdam and Paulsen 1993). In the latter half of the nineteenth century, the railroad brotherhoods attempted to transform their intemperate drinking culture by connecting the temperance message of self-improvement to what it meant to be a "real" railroader. As one leader of the Albuquerque Switchmen's Mutual Aid Association stated in 1891, "What we want is good, sober men, who are upright in their business dealings. Then, we can command the best treatment from both the railroad officials and the business public" (Ducker 1983: 133).

In addition, successful cultural change efforts preserve continuity with the past (Trice and Beyer 1993). The transformation of intemperate drinking cultures occurs when the occupational leadership uses the ritual elements as a lever for reconstructing members' communal sense of self. In the new rituals, however, alcohol as a symbol of communal resistance is transformed into a symbol of the occupational community's destruction, which must be overcome if it is to survive. This is what the railroad brotherhoods sought to accomplish but failed to do in the latter part of the nineteenth century. Within the context of their naturally occurring work rituals, they sought to create an environment in which drinking was seen as inappropriate behavior by disciplining members who drank intemperately on and off the job and by establishing alternative mechanisms for managing work and leisure, e.g., grievance procedures and reading rooms (Ducker 1983). Ultimately, these temperance efforts failed because the leadership of the brotherhoods was half-heartedly committed to temperance. As president of the American Railway Union, Eugene Debs promoted temperance among rail-roaders as the means to creating a strong union; yet he was better known for his drunkenness than his sobriety (Rumbarger 1989). In addition, the violent railroad strikes of the era reinforced and justi-fied, in the minds of many railroaders, their old beliefs about intem-perate drinking as a symbol of resistance and the means to creating communal solidarity (Licht 1983).

Unlike the railroaders, the sandhogs have successfully trans-formed their intemperate drinking culture by incorporating AA's beliefs into their naturally occurring work rituals. The sandhogs control the hiring of work gang members, and gang leaders who are also recovering alcoholics in AA use the hiring process to re-cruit members to the AA belief system. That is, the gang leaders re-cruit sandhogs whom they identify as being alcoholic to the AA program by offering them much-prized employment on the work gangs. Within the context of the gangs, the gang leaders teach them AA's twelve steps to sobriety and communicate that neither individual nor communal survival depends upon their participa-tion in the intemperate drinking rituals. By incorporating the ritu-als of AA into their work lives, the sandhogs are indirectly attacking their old belief that one must drink in order to be a sand-hog and transforming their intemperate drinking culture into a sober one. At the same time, by providing treatment to those whom they define as alcoholic and transforming them into sober workers, they preserve the new belief's continuity with the past by underscoring that members' primary communal obligation is to protect one another.

Intemperate drinking cultures are transformed slowly as, one by one, new members are recruited and socialized into living a temper-ate life. Intemperate drinking slowly loses its symbolic hold over the occupational community, and members relinquish their beliefs about intemperate drinking, including the notion that one must drink in order to be a member of the occupational community. At the same time, however, their naturally occurring work rituals still create strong communal bonding among members. As sandhog gang members, for example, focus on their work and cope with the ever present dangers of tunneling, their interaction continues to produce ritual effects so that members develop a consciousness that is no longer dependent on drinking.

Refreezing

In the refreezing stage, the new temperance beliefs are accepted by community members as the appropriate way to behave and, over time, become taken for granted as truths. In order to become taken for granted, the new beliefs must be continually reinforced if they are to be maintained over time (McAdam, McCarthy, and Zald 1988). This long-term reinforcement takes several forms.

First, like other AA members who are recovering from alcohol, recovering sandhogs seek to maintain their own sobriety by helping other sandhogs still suffering from alcoholism become sober (Rudy 1986; Alcoholics Anonymous 1955). They help them by acting as sober examples for them to follow and by directly instructing them in AA's twelve steps to sobriety. In this way, they demonstrate that one does not have to drink intemperately in order to fulfill one's obligations to community members and thereby reinforce the new temperance beliefs.

Second, as sandhogs have become sober, they have become more involved within the union as gang leaders and union officers. As a result, they now control valuable resources that enable them to reinforce their temperance message throughout the occupational community. In particular, they control the hiring process and recruit only those committed to living a temperate life, either as AA members or as temperate, "social" drinkers.

Third, although the sandhogs have relied upon their alcohol program to transform the community's intemperate drinking culture, they have not confined their message to helping alcoholics. Rather, the underlying mutual aid message of the program is that individual and communal survival depends upon members' helping one another in need. The sandhogs amplify this message by helping community members and their families with a variety of personal problems, including family and emotional difficulties. In addition, the sandhogs have amplified their mutual aid message by helping other unions establish similar programs.

As a result of their reinforcement efforts, the sandhogs are transforming their community so that members now believe that one need not drink intemperately to be a sandhog. Consequently, those sandhogs who are social drinkers do not mix alcohol and work; rather, they drink in a temperate manner, confining their alcohol consumption to their leisure hours. At the same time, those sandhogs who are recovering alcoholics continue to live sober lives and, thus, reinforce the occupational community's new temperance beliefs.

3 *The Sandhogs:*
From Occupational Identity
to Community

*T*he sandhogs are a conservative occupational community of tunnel workers in New York City, whose history reflects members' struggles to build a boundary around their work. In these struggles, the sandhogs make some basic assumptions about their world that guide them in constructing their community: they assume that the world is a very dangerous place and that, in order to survive, they must face those dangers as a tightly knit group. These basic assumptions are deeply embedded within their historical experience, and they are reinforced daily as members live out their lives within the embrace of their occupational community. In this section I first examine the development of these basic assumptions within the context of the sandhogs' efforts to erect and maintain an occupational boundary around their work and then examine how these basic assumptions are reinforced within their communal relationships.

Evolution of the Sandhogs

The assumptions that form the basis of the sandhog community are rooted in the immigrant experience of the nineteenth century and the realities of their work. The sandhogs trace their beginning to the construction of the Brooklyn Bridge in 1870 and the unskilled immigrant laborers hired to build it (Delaney 1983).[1] As unskilled laborers, they were drawn to construction because it required only a strong back and provided them with an opportunity for a fresh start in a new country. Employment on the Brooklyn Bridge, however, provided only an insecure livelihood because there was a surplus pool of unskilled workers and the men could easily be dismissed by their employer. At the same time, working conditions on the project were extremely dangerous. The technologies used to build the bridge were unproven, and the men continuously faced the prospect of instantaneous death or permanent disabilities. Out of these realities, workers soon discovered that their individual survival depended upon being a member of a tightly knit group committed to protecting one another's jobs and lives. These assumptions have emerged out of the sandhogs' struggle to carve out a protected niche in the labor market and have continued to guide them in structuring their relationships.

Emergence of an Occupational Identity

Culture plays a crucial role in the emergence of an occupational community by transforming workers from simply an aggregate of people performing similar tasks into a group with a common identity (Van Maanen and Barley 1984). Although culture is a necessary condition for the emergence of an occupational community, it is not sufficient. In order for an occupational community to develop, the work group must also be able to lay claim to a body of knowledge and skills that set them apart from other work groups, and a labor market for those skills must exist (Freidson 1982).

Occupational cultures often emerge around new technologies and the workers recruited to implement them (Hughes 1958; Gritzer and Arluke 1985; Blum, Roman, and Tootle 1988). As the workers strug-

[1] My description of the sandhog's evolution is drawn from Paul Delaney's (1983) history of the tunnel workers, which was written to commemorate the one hundredth anniversary of the completion of the Brooklyn Bridge. Delaney, a journalist and video producer, also produced the documentary *City without Water*, which publicized the necessity of building Water Tunnel Number 3 to the citizens of New York City.

gle to make sense of their new tasks and surroundings, they begin to develop their own ideas about what they are doing, and they convey these ideas to one another in stories recounting their shared experiences. The immigrant workers recruited to build the Brooklyn Bridge, which was hailed upon its completion as one of the world's greatest engineering feats, used a new and unproven technique for bridge construction, working underwater in compressed air. In order to lay the foundations for the two towers of the bridge, the workers dug out the sand, rocks, and gravel on the bottom of the East River. They accomplished this task by using caissons, large wooden boxes with an open bottom, which were lowered to the river bed and filled with compressed air. After the compressed air pushed the water out of the caissons, the men entered them and dug out the muck. The caissons were extremely large. The one on the Brooklyn side of the bridge measured 168 feet long by 102 feet wide, about half the size of a city block, and weighed 16 million tons; the one on the Manhattan side was even larger.

Working conditions within the caissons were extremely dangerous, and the men experienced the compressed air environment as strange and terrifying. The terror began upon entering the airlock, which was filled with compressed air after the door was closed. As the compressed air rushed in, it made a frightening screech and the men's bodies underwent painful physical changes. Once the air pressures between the airlock and caisson were equalized, a trap door swung open and the men descended through a three-and-a-half foot iron shaft into an eerie underworld. Inside temperatures were always above eighty degrees; the air smelled of human waste because, lacking a toilet, the men defecated where they worked; and few dry spots were to be found. Moreover the men feared instantaneous death from a blowout, that is, compressed air escaping from the caisson and allowing the river waters to rush in. A blowout could be caused by a boulder caught under the caisson's lip as the excavation of the mud and rock allowed the box to descend farther into the river bottom; explosives used to break up the large boulders on the river bottom were also potential sources of blowouts. Fortunately the Great Blowout, which spewed a geyser of water and debris over nearby Fulton Street and instantaneously lowered the Brooklyn caisson a foot, occurred on a Sunday morning when no one was working.

In addition, the men were terrified of contracting caisson's disease (the bends). Although the causes of caisson's disease were unknown at this time, its symptoms are dramatic. It is always painful, often debilitating, and sometimes fatal. As the men dug out the muck and the caissons descended ever deeper toward the river's bedrock, the air pressure within the caissons was increased. At these deeper levels, many men became seriously ill with caisson's disease. Some felt totally debilitated, others experienced wrenching abdominal cramps and broke out into fever accompanied by cold sweats and vomiting. Their chests and joints swelled to twice the normal size; their heads ached from blinding pain.

Working under such new and dangerous conditions, the men began to develop an image of themselves as supermen, uniquely suited to work in what E. F. Farrington, chief mechanic on the Brooklyn Bridge project, described as "Dante's Inferno," where everything took on a weird and unreal appearance:

> There was a confused sensation in the head, like "the rush of many waters." The pulse was at first accelerated, then sometimes fell below the normal rate. The voice sounded faint, unnatural, and it became a great effort to speak. What with the flaming lights, the deep shadows, the confusing noise of hammers, drills, and chains, the half-naked forms flitting about, with here and there a Sisyphus rolling his stone . . . (quoted in Delaney 1983: 2–3)

When such stories reached the surface, New Yorkers also began to think of these immigrant laborers as a race of supermen.

In addition, the men began to develop their own notions about what was required to do their work. They adopted the belief that drinking hard liquor was an essential part of the job because it provided energy for the performance of arduous tasks, protected one against extreme shifts in temperature, and prevented illnesses, particularly caisson's disease. The belief that alcohol enabled one to do hard work was not unique to the immigrants working on the Brooklyn Bridge. Rather, as we saw in Chapter 1, it was well developed among nineteenth-century workmen, and the Brooklyn Bridge laborers adapted it as part of their own belief system.

Although the laborers were beginning to develop an image of themselves as unique and to construct some ideas about how they ought to perform their work, they had no job security. Workers were hired and fired at the whim of the Brooklyn Bridge Company, and the men feared being fired because they could not easily find other work that paid the two dollars a day earned in the caissons. The ease with which workers were fired and replaced is illustrated by the company's efforts to curtail the men's drinking of hard liquor. The company doctor blamed the bends on the workers' poor living conditions and habits, particularly their tendency to spend their off hours in the local saloons, and promulgated nine rules of right living for the men to follow. These rules, which reflected the temperance literature of the time, included eating a meat diet, sleeping eight hours a night, avoiding exposure to the cold, and abstaining from drinking intoxicating liquors. Although these actions proved to be ineffective in preventing the bends, those who failed to observe the clean living rules lost their jobs, and those who came down with the disease were barred from returning to work.

The caissons' hazards and their precarious employment situation fostered the laborers' basic assumptions about work. The world was really a dangerous place, and survival, particularly within the caissons, depended upon watching out for one another's safety. These assumptions hardened into accepted truths as working conditions worsened and men began to die from the bends.

Believing that the company regarded their lives as worthless, the men organized all the crews and, on May 8, 1872, the entire work force walked off the job, protesting hazardous working conditions and inadequate compensation. The strike lasted only three days, but during that time the workers successfully prevented strikebreakers from crossing their picket lines. Ultimately, the men settled for a modest increase in wages and returned to work after the company threatened to fire the whole crew, but they also learned that by standing together they could force their employer to consider their demands for safety. Their euphoria, however, was short-lived because, within a few weeks of the strike settlement, the Brooklyn Bridge Company decided that the hardpan, the extremely hard-packed soil above the bedrock, would be able to support the weight of the Brooklyn tower and laid off all the men.

Although the laborers had begun to develop a work culture, they were slow to develop as an occupational community because no one needed to hire workers skilled in compressed air techniques. The men lacked a permanent labor market for their skills. After the Brooklyn Bridge project closed, two years would elapse before another contractor would discover a use for their skills. In 1874, the Hudson River Railroad Company decided to experiment with compressed air as a technique for building a railroad tunnel under the Hudson River between New York and New Jersey, and they began to recruit men who had worked on the Brooklyn Bridge. The men's experience with the tunneling experiment, however, only deepened their basic assumptions about the realities of compressed air work. Hundreds of men lost their lives to cave-ins, blowouts, and caisson's disease. In July 1880, after a major blowout claimed the lives of twenty laborers, the men threatened to strike over the unsafe conditions. As a result of the accompanying adverse newspaper coverage, the company lost both its financial backers and its public credibility and was forced to abandon the construction of the Hudson tunnels. Once again, the compressed air workers were laid off, but this time, the layoff lasted twenty years.

During the formative years of the sandhogs' occupational community, culture played an important role in transforming the workers from a collection of immigrant laborers into a group with a common destiny. It gave them an identity, a work-based image of themselves as supermen uniquely qualified to deal with the dangers of compressed air work, and it provided the bonds that held them together in their initial efforts to organize for safer working conditions. Because there was no demand for their skills, however, a fully developed occupational community could not emerge during this period.

Solidifying the Boundary

In order for an occupational culture to survive, members must solidify the boundary around their work (Van Maanen and Barley 1984). In addition to a set of shared beliefs and an image around which to organize, this requires that members have a permanent labor market for the knowledge and tasks they claim as their own and recognition from employers that they are uniquely qualified to perform these tasks (Gritzer and Arluke 1985). Such recognition means that the group has been able to solidify its boundaries by excluding nonmembers from performing its claimed tasks within the labor market and a full-fledged occupational community can emerge.

Between 1900 and 1950, a demand for workers with compressed air experience was created, and the workers were able to secure control over that market by the establishment of a union, which ensured that only its members were recruited to do the work. The creation of this labor market became possible because the compressed air technique of tunneling underwater was perfected in other parts of the world and imported back to New York. Using this technique, contractors began over a dozen immense projects between 1900 and 1910, including railroad and subway tunnels under the Hudson and East Rivers of New York City. Subway tunnels under the city's streets and the first of New York's water tunnels were also begun during this period. Despite the hazardous working conditions, these projects attracted thousands of immigrants desperate for work. Work on these projects, however, only deepened the laborers' basic assumptions: the contractors viewed them as expendable, and their survival depended upon standing together.

Unionization is a significant step in the survival of an occupational culture because it solidifies members' control over the market for their skills (Freidson 1982). The Tunnel and Construction Workers Union was born in 1906 when the men organized to protest the dangerous working conditions in the Pennsylvania Railroad tunnels that connected New York City to New Jersey. In order to save $112 a day, the contractor laid off all the airlock tenders, who were responsible for ensuring that the pressure between the airlock and the compressed air environment in the tunnels was correctly maintained. The immediate consequence of this action was a sharp increase in sandhog deaths from the bends, but the contractor remained unalarmed because there was a surplus of immigrant laborers willing to risk their lives for a good day's pay. This situation, however, changed very quickly when the newspapers began reporting the increasing number of deaths in the tunnels and charged the contractor with falsifying evidence in order to cover up his negligence. At the same time, New York City conducted an inquiry into the deaths and concluded that the lack of airlock tenders was a fatal oversight that had caused at least fifty deaths during the first five months of 1906. In addition, the city warned that, if the airlock tenders were not put back to work immediately, more deaths would follow.

As a result of the adverse publicity, the pool of surplus laborers dried up, and the tunnel workers, with the support of such specialized trades as the electricians and explosives experts, some of whose members worked on the compressed air jobs, threatened to strike for the right to organize, the right to safety, and the right to fair pay for dangerous work. On July 30, 1906, five hundred tunnel workers struck the Belmont subway tunnel job, and five thousand men from other trades threatened to walk out in support unless the contractor recognized the Tunnel and Construction Workers Union. Unable to recruit new immigrants who had been frightened off by newspaper accounts, the contractors reluctantly recognized the union and agreed to hire only union labor on all its subway jobs. Over the next ten years, the union fought a series of grueling battles with the contractors, eventually securing its control over all tunnel jobs within the city of New York. In 1917, the union voted to affiliate with the International Hod Carriers, accepting a charter that gave them control over all tunnel jobs in New York and New Jersey and gained job security for its members.

The union was a logical outgrowth of the workers' basic assumptions for it solved the workers' problems of both external adaptation and internal integration. It solved the problem of external adaptation by forcing the contractors to recognize the union's right to bargain collectively for community members, and it solved the problem of internal integration by demonstrating to workers that by sticking together they could gain control over their employment and working conditions.

Throughout the first half of this century, the sandhogs' community remained highly stable because there was a long-term labor market for their knowledge and skills. During this period, they constructed some of New York's most important infrastructures, including the Holland, Lincoln, and Midtown Tunnels and the city's labyrinth of subway and sewer systems. Among the most important projects were the city's water tunnels. Historically, water has been a scarce resource in New York City, and there had been many schemes, some honest and others outright fraudulent, for bringing water to its teeming populace. Water Tunnel Number 1 was begun in 1907 and completed in 1917. Under state legislation, the city condemned and submerged nine villages in the Catskill Mountains in order to construct four reservoirs: Schoharie, Ashokan, Kensico, and

Hillview. From the reservoirs, Water Tunnel Number 1 runs 1,114 feet under the Hudson River and reaches depths of 750 feet under the city as it flows from the Bronx through Manhattan to its terminus in Brooklyn. Water Tunnel Number 2, completed in 1937, connects New York City to the Delaware Reservoir System. Within the city, the tunnel runs through the Bronx and Queens to its terminus in Brooklyn.

The sandhogs were able to solidify their occupational boundary because, during the first part of the twentieth century, a labor market developed for their tunneling skills and, by unionizing, they were able to force the contractors to hire only occupational members. In addition, the processes of unionizing and fighting for safer working conditions deepened the sandhogs' commitment to their basic assumptions: that the world is dangerous, and survival depends upon being part of a tightly knit group. Consequently, the occupational boundary the sandhogs erected around their work was very tightly drawn to exclude nonmembers and to subject individual members to the community's collective will. During the past few decades, however, the sandhogs' cultural assumptions and occupational boundary would be sorely tested.

Struggle to Maintain the Boundary

Occupational communities, faced with changing labor markets and new technologies, must struggle to preserve their cultures and maintain their boundaries. The survival of an occupational culture depends upon both a dependable market for workers' skills and the ability to ensure that only community members are able to perform those jobs. Throughout the first half of this century, both conditions existed for the sandhogs: tunneling jobs were plentiful, and the union was able to control its labor market. During the fifties, however, employment conditions changed drastically because New York began to run out of tunnel projects and contractors began introducing new technologies into the work processes. The introduction of the "mole," a tunneling machine, reduced the size of the crew working on the face of the tunnel from thirty-six to ten men and the use of air-driven power wrenches reduced the time necessary for tightening bolts from an hour to twenty minutes. As a result, many sandhogs, who were unable to find work on the few remaining tunnels, began to leave the union in search of other kinds of jobs.

With the collapse of its labor market, the sandhogs once again faced the possible extinction of their occupational community. The labor market's collapse did not affect the sandhogs' basic assumptions about their work; however, in order to ensure their survival, they were forced to rethink how they enacted those beliefs. In order to tighten up their relationships with one another, the union introduced two innovations intended to renew members' commitment to the community. First, in order to protect the jobs of local members, the union closed their books to the drifters, those men who, in hard times, would drop their membership, drift into other lines of work, and return to sandhogging when a new project was started. The local men did not regard the drifters as real sandhogs. Second, the union introduced a welfare and pension fund, requiring all members to contribute 2 percent of their salary in order to aid those out of work and to ensure that retired members had financial support. In order to solve the problem of external adaptation, the union adopted a proactive stance. When the contractors, in the fifties, attempted to hire nonunion workers in the tunnels, the sandhogs fought them and won. They also lobbied the city council to appropriate funds for a third water tunnel, arguing that it was necessary in order to shut down and repair Water Tunnels Number 1 and 2, which were now leaking badly because of aging. The new water tunnel would ensure them years of employment.

In 1961, Mayor Robert F. Wagner ensured, at least temporarily, the survival of the sandhogs' culture when he proposed the construction of Water Tunnel Number 3, a project billed as the largest nonmilitary project in history and estimated to be completed around the year 2020. The first stage of Water Tunnel Number 3, which was finally begun in 1970, includes a huge underground distribution chamber at Van Cortland Park in the Bronx. The chamber is twenty-five stories deep and contains a series of valves for shunting water between the old Water Tunnels, Numbers 1 and 2, and the new Number 3. From the chamber, Tunnel 3, a hole that is bored through a deep bedrock and is lined with concrete and steel rings, runs south through the Bronx into Manhattan where it cuts across 78th Street and under the East River before reaching its terminus in Queens. Stage 2 will tunnel down Manhattan and terminate at Battery Park.

Stage 3 will run through Queens and terminate in Brooklyn. Stage 4 will run under New York Harbor from Manhattan to Staten Island. Water Tunnel Number 3 is vital to the survival of both the City of New York and the sandhogs. It is vital to the city because the other two tunnels are leaking badly and will need to be shut down and drained for inspection and repairs to prevent them from collapsing. Engineering experts fear that, if something should happen to either tunnel before Tunnel 3 is completed, much of the city could be without water for up to a year. In this worst-case scenario, toilets would not work, fires would rage out of control, and New York's economy would go bust. Rolf Eliassen, an independent engineer at Stanford University, examined the state of the tunnels in 1973 and concluded: "One can only hope and pray that no major conflagration will occur in the meantime and that city Tunnels No. 1 and 2 will continue to function despite their age and no opportunity for maintenance" (quoted in Delaney 1983: 49). The tunnel is vital to the sandhog community because it is the only remaining large-scale construction job in the New York City area that requires their unique skills. Without this work, the sandhogs might not survive into the next century.

Despite the importance of Water Tunnel Number 3 to the city, the project has been plagued with delays due to city, state, and federal government financial problems. The first stage was shut down in 1975 because of a dispute between the contractors and the city. The city, short of cash because it had been spending its capital expenditure funds on day-to-day expenses, saw the dispute as an ideal time to shut the tunnel down completely. In order to get the project restarted, the sandhogs made their cause public by suing both the city and the contractors and by taking the story of New York's threatened water supply to the media, state and federal legislators, and the business community.

The sandhogs' politicking paid off. In 1977, new contracts were signed, and the number of sandhogs back at work had grown from forty to seven hundred. Finally, in 1983, the contracts to complete the first stage of Water Tunnel Number 3 were signed. Full employment, however, was short-lived. By 1988, the number of men working to complete the first stage had sunk below three hundred; in 1989, the first stage was completed.

Since completion of the first stage, the union has continued to lobby city, state, and federal legislators for financial support for the completion of Water Tunnel Number 3. While waiting for the second phase to begin, a few dozen union members built a small tunnel on Staten Island; most, however, left the union for other types of work. Some have found work in other construction trades; some have found work outside the construction industry; and many continue to struggle, putting together whatever odd jobs are available in order to survive. Fortunately, in 1993, the second phase of Tunnel 3 was finally begun and by early 1994, a hundred sandhogs were back working in the tunnels.

For the sandhogs, the world of work remains a very dangerous place, and they continue to believe that their survival depends upon the solidarity of their communal life. These basic assumptions are deeply rooted within the historical transformation of their occupational culture. Guided by these basic assumptions, the sandhogs have constructed a conservative occupational community, which places primary emphasis upon preserving the group. Today, in the face of a changed labor market and the introduction of new technologies into the tunnels, they struggle to maintain their occupational community and preserve their culture.

From Occupational Identity to Community: Communal Bonding

Despite their economic hardships, the sandhogs remain highly committed to their occupational culture because their work role means more than simply making a living. They regard it as the basis of a communal life, building their sense of self and their entire lives around it so that they come to feel incomplete when not working with and spending time with other sandhogs. This sentiment is aptly expressed by one sandhog: "I've worked at everything, but anytime there was a sandhog job I'd come back to it. . . . I don't know what the hell it is that brings a guy back to the tunnels. A lot of times a guy will be working outside, making good money in a healthier environment. But, if a tunnel starts, he's back to the tunnel."[2]

The sandhogs' shared work experiences promote the communal bonding so essential to preserving their occupational community.

---

[2] This and all other unattributed quotations come from the author's fieldwork.

Members of occupational communities build their sense of self around their work role, take members of the occupational community as their primary reference group, and, preferring to spend time with their own kind, integrate their work and leisure activities (Salaman 1974; Van Maanen and Barley 1984). Communal bonding contributes to the preservation of the sandhog culture because it reinforces the sandhogs' basic assumptions about themselves and their work environment. In this section, I examine the factors that promote communal bonding within the sandhog community.

The primary determinant of workers' developing strong communal bonds is involvement in work (Salaman 1974). People who are emotionally engaged in their work are likely to build their sense of self around their occupational role, take their coworkers as the primary reference group for their values, and prefer to spend their leisure time with their work mates. Several characteristics of tunnel work heavily engage the sandhogs, prompting them to build strong communal bonds among themselves: Exercising control over work, sharing strong emotions, and structural factors which encourage workers to meld work and leisure activities.

Work Control

Workers who exercise control over the performance of their tasks become highly involved with their work and develop strong communal bonds with one another (Salaman 1974; Van Mannen and Barley 1984). Indeed, the necessity for workers to cope with the uncertainties of dangerous conditions such as those found in mining leads them to seek the means of exerting control over their work by banding together. For the sandhogs, the hog house, a large corrugated-metal building situated at the entrance to the tunnel, symbolizes their control over their work and their distinctiveness from other occupations. They speak of it in glowing terms. "Other unions don't have such facilities; it makes us unique!" The hog house is the hub of their work lives, their command center. Here, they "saddle up" before each shift, exchanging their street clothes for their miner's costume: layered, well-worn, often patched dungarees and work shirts topped off by a scarred, battered hard hat with a miner's light, a yellow waist-length rain slicker, and knee-high yellow boots. It is the place to which they return after each shift with their work mates to wash away the dirt, grime, and pain of the tunnels and to recount the day's adventures. It is also the place where unemployed members come to look for work and to pass the day when no work is available. Inside the hog house are rows of lockers with neatly aligned benches, a shower, a counter area with a pot of coffee continuously brewing, other beverages and snacks, and sturdy tables for eating and playing cards. To the uninitiated, it is a filthy place with wet and mud-encrusted clothes suspended overhead on pulleys and a locker-room stench of sweaty socks. To the sandhogs, however, it is a sacred place, strictly off-limits to outsiders.

The sandhogs, like other craft unions, are responsible for hiring, training, evaluating, and firing members (Stinchcombe 1959; Silver 1986; Riemer 1979, 1982); consequently, they feel an intense loyalty to their union rather than to the contractors who employ them. Contractors bid for and win contracts. The union, however, hires and fires workers, and it exercises this control through a hierarchy of union members. On every tunnel job, there is a walking boss and a foreman who make sure the contractor's orders are fulfilled but who are themselves union members. Under them are stewards, who see that the union contract is obeyed, and then the gang leaders.

In sandhogging, life revolves around the gang, the union's basic work unit, which exerts day-to-day control over members' activities; individuals develop exceptionally strong bonds with the members of their gang. The gang is responsible for hiring, training, disciplining, and firing members, and each gang on a crew performs a special task. When a new job starts, the foreman often hires members he knows. Sandhogs are hired on a gang for the duration of a particular job; if there is more work than members can handle, nonunion members are temporarily recruited to fill out the gangs. Some gangs are relatively short-lived; others, like the "bull gang," which cleans up after the others and is the last to leave the tunnel, can assure members of steady work for years. If a gang member is absent, his place will be filled by someone else; if he is absent for more than three days without just cause, he loses his position to the person who filled it. This filling in is called "shaping," and it occurs before each shift. Generally, those who are unemployed and hope to get on a gang arrive at the hog house early for shaping; many of those unable to get on a gang that day will also hang out at the hog house drinking, talking, and playing cards from one shift to the next.

Once on a gang, a person is not likely to be fired. On occasion, however, a foreman does fire a worker. Generally this happens when, in the estimation of the gang members, someone is not pulling their own weight.

If he just didn't want to work and was lazy, they [the foreman] would just fire him. If he did something that was dangerous to the gang, there'd be a good chance someone [a gang member] would kick his ass, and [the foreman] would fire him. Definitely! Especially if it's something that's done out of stupidity or laziness or unconcern for the other workers. They [the gang members] don't tolerate it.

Although the foreman does the hiring and firing, it is the gang members in evaluating day-to-day performance of workers who exercise control. If gang members, for instance, believe someone is lazy or dangerous, the gang will not recruit them: "Some people shape and just don't get on steady. They end up steady shapers. If things are very busy someone will put them on, but they're not really wanted [by the gang]. . . . Not that they couldn't be good workers. They don't have the desire to be, and they're looking to milk the money." This structure fosters an intense gossip network about who is and is not working, where the work is, and which gangs are shaping.

Gangs also promote involvement in work and strong communal bonds because they are the primary way in which newcomers are socialized (e.g., Van Maanen 1973; Vaught and Smith 1980). There is no formal apprenticeship program in the Tunnel and Construction Workers Union; the only way to learn sandhogging is in the gangs. Newcomers learn the trade by observing, following orders, and asking questions of the more experienced miners in the gangs. The first lesson taught to newcomers by gang members is to protect one another from the tunnel's physical dangers. Gradually, newcomers may learn the intricacies of a specific job, such as "doing a burn" so that when dynamited, the rock will break where it is supposed to. Most sandhogs, however, learn to do whatever is required to construct a tunnel safely.

Within the sandhog community, exercising control over one's work promotes communal bonding because, through the gang, individuals become intensely involved with their work. The gang is the individual sandhog's life line, and he becomes intensely involved with it. As a newcomer, the gang teaches him the techniques of tunneling as well as his obligations to the members of his gang. Within its embrace, he develops a sensitivity to dangerous situations, the critical sixth sense enabling him and his fellow gang members to survive in the tunnels. It provides him regular employment so long as he pulls his weight and works safely. Those who violate these obligations, however, are treated harshly, fired from the gang, and eventually ejected from the sandhog community.

Sharing Strong Work-Related Emotions

The sharing of strong work-related emotions also promotes involvement with work and the development of communal bonding (Salaman 1974; Trice 1993). Such emotions include playfulness, pride of craftsmanship, and a sense of marginality. But the most powerful shared emotion predicting communal bonding is the fear associated with danger on the job.

Dangerous working conditions lead people to become highly involved with their occupational role (Haas 1977; Van Maanen 1980; Fitzpatrick 1980). Consequently, mining, which is particularly dangerous, leads miners all over the world to construct strong communal bonds with one another (Dennis, Henriques, and Slaughter 1969; Gouldner 1954; Fitzpatrick 1980; Vaught and Smith 1980). As in other forms of mining, danger is a pervasive theme in the sandhog community because it is a reality: statistically, for every mile of tunnel, one sandhog dies. Each year Father Considine of the St. Barnabas Church in the North Bronx conducts a mass to remember those killed in the tunnels, and a plaque honoring them hangs prominently in the front of the union hall, underscoring the ever-present danger with which they must cope and reinforcing their basic assumptions.

To the sandhogs, the tunnels symbolize the dangerous life they share and the obligations they owe one another. They describe the tunnels as "another world" unintelligible to outsiders, and they underscore that individual survival inside the tunnels depends upon being part of a crew whose members watch out for one another. One sandhog describes the tunnels as "something out of *Star Wars* or a James Bond movie with all these guys walking around in their yellow suits and the heavy equipment." As if to signal the hazards of this other world, the crew's mood shifts from high jinks to high seriousness when they enter the tunnels. Inside, the air hangs heavy, full of diesel fumes and dust particles from the crushed rock. The tunnels, hundreds of feet below the surface and many miles long, vary in size from twenty to thirty feet in diameter. Once down there, the men, particularly those working many miles from the entrance, will not come out until the end of their shift. Conditions at the face of the tunnel are so dirty and dusty the men can barely see beyond a few feet and they must be ever alert to the dangers of newly blasted rock and heavy equipment such as the jumbo drill and the mucker. The men say, "This is very isolating, being so out of touch with the rest of the world. That is why trust in the gang is so essential."

An accident in June 1982, illustrates the danger of the tunnels and the obligations the sandhogs feel toward one another:

We heard an engineer up the line blowing his air horn. Apparently an agitator [concrete mixer on a rail car] had gotten loose. . . . When I heard the air horn I knew something was wrong and I got my men off the track just in time to see these agitators shoot by with no motor behind. We knew there were men working down the line about a mile and a half, and all I could visualize was bodies all over the place once this thing hit. I ran back the line about a thousand feet, picked up the phone to warn them, but at the time they had men working through lunch drilling, and they couldn't hear the phone ringing. By the time they did, it was too late. The agitators just plowed into two high cars— scaffold work on tracks, plus the concrete pump. . . . Nobody got killed, thank God. When we got them out of the hole, seven men were badly injured. One man lost his leg, and the other leg is still in jeopardy. To get him out, . . . we had to cut part of his foot off, because he was wrapped around a pipe. . . . We took our time, cut the skin off that was wrapped around the coupling. . . . The people with broken arms and broken legs didn't even know they had them. They were out there helping everybody else get out, carrying stretchers. When it comes to accidents, they're all professionals down there. (quoted in Delaney 1983: 64–65)

Another accident on November 24, 1992, provides additional evidence of the sandhogs' dangerous working conditions. A sixteen-ton winch fell 503 feet into one of the shafts being dug for the construction of Stage 2 of Water Tunnel Number 3. As the winch ricocheted off the walls, it knocked down scaffolding, killing one sandhog and injuring seven others. One survivor recounted his story:

> I was on a ladder. . . . I just saw sparks and heard an explosion. The next thing I know the ladder I was on was gone. The decks were gone. I was hanging by my finger tips. I thought I couldn't hold on. . . . I thought of my two kids. And, somehow, I managed the strength to turn around, get my fingers in a grating, pull myself up to a cable and then jump on to the side [where I clung to the shaft's steel molding until help arrived]. (Jones 1993: B3)

The first lesson the new tunnel worker learns from his gang is that sandhogging is dangerous and every member must look out for one another. Any hard feelings between individuals are forgotten in the tunnel, and this norm is reinforced by heroic stories of sandhogs' risking their lives to save one another. As one sandhog explained to me, they develop a sixth sense about trouble in the tunnels:

> People really look out for one another. . . . They get a sense when something is going to happen. . . . We were pulling down the cribbing up on top of the tunnel, and I was standing on the muck cars. We were pulling up rail as we went, and we had the rail up on top of the mucker. . . . My leg went down in between the rails, and I was falling sideways over the mucker. . . . Luckily, [Pete] was there and grabbed me by the shoulders and pushed me back up before the leg just snapped. It gets like a sixth sense. . . . That's the way you get. There's a real caring down there. Maybe some of the people don't get along together . . . but once the work day begins all of that goes out the window.

Similarly, one sandhog, directing a 650-pound dynamite blast on Stage 2 of the water tunnel project, commented while anxiously watching the members of his gang leave the shaft before detonating the explosion: "I'm responsible for these men and, thank God, knock on wood, I've never hurt one in my life or had one get hurt working with me. And I don't want to start now" (quoted in Collison 1994).

Danger promotes communal bonding. The hazardous working conditions in the tunnels dramatically underscore the workers' shared existence and the obligations they owe one another. There is "a real caring down there" that unites them in a life-and-death struggle with the tunnels. Consequently, individual crew members are compelled by their occupational community to put their differences aside upon entering the tunnels and act in one another's behalf.

In addition to danger, the sandhogs share three other strong work-related affects that promote communal bonding: playfulness, pride in their work, and a feeling that the outside world devalues them. Playfulness at work heightens workers' involvement and promotes bonding (Roy 1960), and the sandhogs experience their work world as playful. On and off the job, there is a great deal of good-natured ribbing and horseplay. Some of this joking is done to reinforce the lessons miners need to learn on the job. Frequently it is easier to joke with someone about their mistakes than to confront them squarely, but practical jokes also serve as a means of testing newcomers to see whether they will control their temper and fit into the gang. Among dynamiters, for instance,

> there is a lot of ball breaking. . . . You get a terrible headache as you break sticks off and the nitroglycerin gets into the skin. . . . When I first went down, a long time ago, one of the old timers told me that you could break off a stick of dynamite and rub it around the inside of your helmet before you put it on your head, and that would stop the headaches. Actually what it did was make the headaches ten times worse.

Playfulness is also evident in the stories they gleefully recount about drinking and fighting. *The New York Times* of March 12, 1907, reported a sandhog party celebrating the opening of the Morton Street PATH tube.

> The Sandhog Band appeared on the stage and made more noise than sixteen calliopes. The Sandhogs wore their yellow oilskin suits with long rubber boots and yellow tunneling hats. Instead

of playing upon brass instruments, they had trombones, coronets, and other instruments made of tin. . . . From the tuba came a bubbling sound like that of a compressed air blow-out under the river. The tin coronet wailed as mournfully as a fog siren, but the brass horn produced a noise that sounded like a tunnel explosion. [When the band began to play], folks along Fifth Avenue became frightened and the [police came to see what was happening]. . . . Within a few minutes that place was in an uproar with four hundred miners pelting the Sandhog Band with loaves of bread, chunks of beef and other things handy at the tables. The army of waiters became frightened and fled pell mell. (quoted in Delaney 1983: 16–17)

Workers who meld their work and leisure also develop strong communal bonds with one another (Salaman 1974; Gamst 1980). The integration of work and leisure among sandhogs is aptly described by the following remark:

There's a lot of camaraderie among workers. . . . A lot of joking and kidding around . . . a lot of socializing off the job, people going to each other's weddings, parties, and social events. They see each other on a social basis more than most other trades. . . . It's a lot like a family, many of them have known each other for twenty, thirty years. They've been through a lot of bad times together—been through a lot of good times together. They are very close.

Pride in one's work also enhances involvement and promotes communal bonding (Salaman 1974; Gamst 1980); the sandhogs take great pride in their craftsmanship and sweat labor. When asked what it means to be a sandhog, members invariably reply that they are proud of their hard work and craftsmanship.

The word itself gives them a lot of pride. They enjoy being sandhogs. . . . It's not the money; they get a lot of pride out of what they do. . . . Sandhogs take great pride in how much work they can do. They actually go down there and try to outdo the craziest gang. . . . If they hear so and so shot two loads of dynamite and mucked out twice, they are down there trying to shoot three loads of dynamite.

There is a popular sandhog story about how some sandhogs, who were working on San Francisco's subway, broke the California crew's rate for putting in steel rings. When building a tunnel, they dig out the rock and put in steel rings to hold up the earth. After putting in five or six rings, they pour concrete around it. The California crew did one ring a day, but the sandhogs did two or three rings a day "to prove that they were the hardest working, toughest guys around." Not surprisingly, then, the sandhogs regard themselves as among the finest miners in the world.

The sandhogs also take great pride in knowing that their tunnels will be used by New Yorkers for generations to come. As one worker, commenting on Water Tunnel Number 3, put it: "Every time I would go down and I would work my eight hours and I would say, 'Well, I've made my contribution.' . . . People will be able to enjoy it in future years. . . . Even after I have died and gone it will still be there because we are doing something New York City will always have for the duration" (quoted in Collison 1994).

Workers who sense that the rest of society does not value their work also become highly involved with their work and build strong communal bonds with one another because they believe that no one else really understands them (Salaman 1974; Searle-Chatterjee 1979). Although the sandhogs take great pride in their work, they feel that the rest of society places little value upon their labor. This is not unusual because society generally regards mining as a dirty and low-status occupation (Hodge, Siegel, and Rossi 1972; Gouldner 1954; Seidman et al. 1958), and this attitude is reflected in how the sandhogs feel about themselves. As one sandhog relative described it, they feel like the "worms of society," laboring in a subterranean labyrinth at tasks unimaginable to the average person, who only sees the dirt. Indeed, the sandhogs point with pride to their tunnels, which form a basic component of the infrastructure of New York City's economy. They also point to the necessity of Water Tunnel Number 3 to the city's survival. Despite such accomplishments, however, they conclude that other people do not and cannot understand what it means to be a sandhog. How could it be otherwise? How could anyone who has not spent time in the tunnels know what it is like to be confined in this dangerous space, isolated for hours on end from the rest of the world? Only other sandhogs can really know what such work is like and understand what it means to be a sandhog. Because no one else really understands, they prefer to spend their leisure time with other sandhogs, where their prideful talk about their work will be correctly interpreted.

While playfulness makes even the dullest work engrossing (Roy 1960), the sandhogs, like other miners (Vaught and Smith 1980), use it to test newcomers, reinforce the lessons everyone must know to survive in the tunnels, and generally smooth over difficult relationships with one another. Similarly, the sandhogs' pride in their craftsmanship underscores their distinctiveness from other workers who do not have what it takes to survive in the tunnels and makes them feel uniquely privileged to be sandhogs. In the end, however, the sandhogs are driven to integrate their work and leisure because the rest of society does not really understand who they are or the value of what they do.

Structural Features of Work Related to Bonding

Three structural features prompt workers to meld their work and leisure lives: kinship-based recruitment into the occupation (e.g., Barley 1983; Miller and Van Maanen 1982); geographic concentration (e.g., Niederhoffer and Niederhoffer 1968; Hill 1981); and shift work (e.g., Cottrell 1934, 1940; Smith 1972). All three structural features also prompt the sandhogs to integrate their work and leisure lives and develop strong communal bonds with one another.

Because the sandhogs are a father-son union, there has always been a great deal of interaction among members off as well as on the job. Traditionally, sandhogging attracted immigrant Irish and later also West Indian laborers, two groups who settled in their own ethnic neighborhoods and passed their occupation from father to son.[3] Consequently, the sons of sandhogs grew up together, attending school, going to church, and dreaming of becoming sandhogs. On the job, sandhogs were known by their neighborhoods: Bronx Irish-American, Brooklyn Irish-American, or Bronx-Donegal man, West Indian Philadelphian or New York City blacks. Today, Irish surnames and West Indian accents remain common; and newly arrived immigrants ("green horns") continue to find sandhog work through relatives. In recent years, however, these old geographic enclaves

---

[3] The sandhogs are proud of the fact that they were the first union to be racially integrated in New York City.

have begun to break down. Prompted by deteriorating inner city housing and increasing income, many sandhogs have moved to the suburbs in search of better living conditions. But in many instances, the sandhogs moved close to one another in the suburbs so that they could maintain their old relationships. They can still see one another in their leisure time and continue to share rides to and from work. Increasingly, however, the boundaries of the sandhog community are marked by their consciousness of kind rather than by geographic neighborhoods.

Shift work also prompts the sandhogs to integrate their work and leisure and develop strong communal bonds. Some gangs may work the morning shift; others may work on the graveyard. This situation means that the sandhogs cannot establish routinized schedules that fit in with those of other workers in other occupations; consequently, they end up spending their leisure time with other sandhogs.

The Sandhog Sense of Self and Occupational Community

The sandhog sense of self is a reflection of the occupational community's basic assumptions: the world is a very dangerous place, and survival depends upon facing those dangers as a strongly bonded group. Involvement with work and the structural features that promote the integration of work and leisure prompt the sandhogs to build their lives around their occupational self and to look to one another as their primary reference group for values. The individual self is a reflection of their collective self-image, and the individual's relationship to the rest of the world reflects the occupation's orientation to the larger society. Individuals are above all sandhogs, and their primary obligations are to preserving the group in a very dangerous world.

Ever since the first stories began circulating about the weird environment and hazardous conditions in the Brooklyn Bridge caissons, people have envisioned the sandhogs as a race of supermen doing dirty work. Not surprisingly, then, the sandhogs also think of themselves as possessing special qualities that enable them to work in the tunnels. Repeatedly, sandhogs say that "everyone isn't suited to this work. Lots of guys try it but they don't last. They just can't hack it."

The sandhog self is also a hard-working, fun-loving, craftsman who is intensely proud of his sweat labor and generous toward his peers. For instance, Alfie E. is a legend regarded as a two-fisted fighter with a kind heart, a superb craftsman capable of building any kind of tunnel, and numerous stories circulate about his readiness to settle disputes with his fists and his generosity to other sandhogs.

> He is probably the biggest living legend within the sandhogs. A tough, tough guy who could build any kind of tunnel. He really knew what he was doing. . . . One time we were putting in steel rings and he wanted the ring flush against the rock. [Smitty] said it wouldn't go back any further. [Alfie] put [Smitty's] arm behind the ring and told him he was going to hit it with a sledgehammer and he'd better hope that it didn't move. They got the job done right. . . . [Another time], when we would start a tunnel Father Carey would come down and say mass. . . . They all knelt down except this one guy who was standing up with his head up. [Alfie] knocked him out and said to Father Carey, "You'll have to excuse this guy. He's got no fuckin' manners." . . . On the 63rd Street job . . . I would say he knocked out fifty people. . . . I mean one punch is all it took. By the same token, if someone had family troubles or was hurt or couldn't work, he made sure they got paid. If somebody's wife had to go into the hospital, he had a thousand dollar check there for him. He was just really a good, good man.

Within the sandhog culture, people are referred to by nicknames conferred upon them by the community. Nicknames, in addition to symbolizing one's membership, highlight the community's hold over the whole person and signify its distinctiveness from the outside world (Vaught and Smith 1980; Lucas 1969). Sometimes these are affectionate names of childhood so that even in middle age one is known as Joey, Billy, Bobby, Mickey, Sammy, or Jimmy. Often, however, the group's nickname for someone is derived from some mistake made by, or stunt pulled by, the individual when he was first hired or some peculiar trait or characteristic of the individual: such monikers as Blowout Bill, Big Nose, Agitator Al, and Dynamite Dan reinforce their identity with the community.

The sandhogs look to one another as their primary reference group because they feel that no one else can understand what it means to be a sandhog. In looking to one another, they learn that their primary obligation is to preserving their communal life. Within the gangs, they learn that doing a good job means putting in a full day's work and not shirking their duties. "That doesn't mean everyone carries two hundred pounds. A good foreman utilizes the capabilities of all the men on the gang. Some are strong and others are quick and agile under stuff. It means that the gang member is suppose to do his work and, if he doesn't, the gang will get rid of him." Most of all, they learn from the oft-repeated stories that their primary obligation is to protect one another in the tunnels.

Obligations in the gang extend to protecting the sandhogs' work and doing whatever is necessary to hold the line against incursions by other workers. A story about a construction company that attempted to break the union exemplifies their commitment to preserving their occupational community.

> They came in the late fifties. They were going to break the New York unions. . . . [We told them that] the ones who were going to build tunnels in New York were sandhogs. They insisted they weren't going to hire union guys and brought in all these guys from out of state. Then we went up there and wrecked their hog houses and wrecked the bosses. Put the bosses in the hospital and burned down their offices. So they more or less thought they might have to hire union help.

Today, protection of the union means paying dues into its political action fund and spreading the word about the necessity to complete Water Tunnel Number 3.

Conclusion

An occupational culture is a pattern of shared meanings intended to ensure group survival. These shared meanings are basic assumptions that members make about their relationship to one another and their environment. Basic assumptions are socially constructed as workers struggle to make sense of their world; those beliefs that are verified by experience are passed on to future generations who reconstruct them within the context of their own historical circumstances.

The sandhogs are a conservative occupational community. They assume that their world is a very dangerous place and that their survival is dependent upon facing those dangers as a strongly bonded group. These beliefs grew out of their hazardous experiences within the tunnels and a fickle labor market. In attempting to cope with these circumstances, they learned that survival in the tunnels required looking out for one's crew members and that survival within the labor market required creating and maintaining a strong craft union. Down in the tunnels and within the union, the sandhogs reinforce these beliefs in their daily interactions and in their struggle to maintain their occupational boundaries.

Strong communal bonds are an essential ingredient in preserving the sandhogs' boundaries and, thus, their occupational culture, because they promote a consciousness of kind as well as of differences from the outside world. The primary determinant of strong communal bonds is high involvement with one's work. Several factors make sandhogging engrossing: the control the union and gangs exert over tunneling and the sharing of strong work-related emotions, especially the sense of danger, playfulness, pride of craftsmanship and a feeling of marginality. Secondary determinants of strong communal bonding are those structural features of sandhogging that prompt members to meld their work and leisure activities: The sandhogs are a father-son union, and tunneling is done in shifts, which means that sandhogs are often working when the rest of the world is at leisure.

Strong communal bonding prompts members to take sandhogging as their primary identity and build their sense of self around their work role. Consequently, their individual self is a reflection of their collective self-image and orientation toward the outside world. They are above all else sandhogs, and their primary obligation is to preserve the occupational community in a very dangerous world. Thus, the sandhog self incorporates the community's basic assumptions about occupational members to one another and the outside world. In the chapter that follows, I shall examine how drinking rituals reinforced the sandhogs' sense of community by enhancing their communal bonds and further highlighting their occupational boundary.

4   Sandhogging and Intemperate Drinking

*T*hroughout the world, mining is associated with distinctive drinking behaviors. Distinctive drinking cultures, for example, are found in the mines of Eastern Europe (Apostolov 1971; Poleksic 1969), France (Bresard and Gomberaux 1962), England (Dennis, Henriques, and Slaughter 1969), Bolivia (Taussig 1980; Nash 1979), and the United States (Gouldner 1954; Staudenmeier 1985; Lantz 1958). Within these diverse ethnic communities, drinking means something more than the consumption of beverage alcohol. It reflects miners' concerns with group solidarity and safety.

In Bolivia, for example, drinking is associated with the ancient belief that the tin ores are a living substance replenishable by the devil after receiving periodic libations (Nash 1979). In order to placate the devil, the miners periodically enact a ceremony called the "ch'alla," the clinching of a deal over a drink (Taussig 1980). In this ceremony, Tio, the devil, is offered alcohol, coca, and cigarettes so that he will supply ore and provide the miners with safe passage. At the same time, the ch'alla, like other rituals, enhances the miners' feelings of solidarity by highlighting the common life shared by the group and the obligations owed to one another. Although the Bolivian ch'alla may seem somehow primitive in today's high-tech world, it is not far removed from the sandhog practice before the opening of a new tunnel of saying a Catholic mass, in which they pray for their safe delivery and consume communal wine.

Since the seventies, the sandhogs have been transforming their intemperate drinking. In the seventies, they accepted drinking on the job as common practice and, melding their leisure and work lives, encouraged often-heavy drinking with gang members after work. Today, their drinking culture has been transformed into a temperate one. They no longer drink on the job, and when melding leisure and work lives, they emphasize moderate drinking or abstinence.

The drinking rituals of the sandhogs' earlier culture reinforced their sense of community by promoting feelings of group solidarity and symbolically marking communal boundaries. Sandhog drinking had all of the elements of ritual (Collins 1988): it occurred within the group, especially the gangs; it focused the individual's attention on shared communal experiences, particularly the consumption of alcohol; and it reinforced the common emotions shared by gang members in their work. Drinking was a potent symbol of the sandhogs' communal life, highlighting the basic assumptions they make about work life: the world is a very dangerous place, and occupational survival depends upon facing that hostile world as a strongly bonded group. Drinking rituals defined who was a member of the community and the obligations that insiders owed to one another. As the sandhogs poignantly put it, "You cannot be a miner unless you drink!"

Drinking in the Sandhog Community

Ceremonial drinking constructs an ideal world; that is, communal members use drinking rituals to make sense of the chaotic world around them (Douglas 1987). Historically, the sandhogs have used drinking to strengthen the symbolic boundary around their community and, thus, further distinguish themselves from outsiders. Sandhogs drank. They drank with one another, and their intemperate drinking marked them as being disreputable within the context of American drinking practices. Even today, the sandhogs are regarded by the larger society as being disreputable because they are perceived to drink irresponsibly. This perception is reflected in the words other workers use to describe them. When I told a staff member of the Central Labor Council that I was writing about the sand-hogs, he laughed and replied, "They are a bunch of drunks." Not surprisingly, the sandhogs felt a sense of marginality, living at the edge of respectable American society.

The sandhogs' intemperate drinking culture was related to the the Irish heritage of many tunnel workers. The Irish were one of the first European immigrant groups to arrive in the United States and consequently one of the first to experience the wrath of the temper-ance movement (Lender and Martin 1987). The Irish were described as being dirty, lazy, rowdy, and ill-mannered, but most of all, they were characterized as drunkards. For them, drinking took on new meaning; it became a way of asserting one's ethnic identity. Hard drinking made one more Irish and distinguished one from other ethnic groups. In reaffirming one's Irishness, drinking became a sa-cred symbol of the group:

> In Ireland drinking had been a consequence of communal con-viviality; now in America, it had become the mystical means of community, creating an imaginary community to fill the void where a real one had once stood. . . . Hard drinking had all the appearances of a religious obligation—the obligation to be Irish and promote one's Irishness. The implication was the more one drank, the more Irish one became. (Stivers 1985: 115–16)

Drinking, as we saw in Chapter 3, was a common practice on the first sandhog project, the Brooklyn Bridge, and the custom has been passed on, along with the job, through generations of sandhogs from father to son. The sandhogs, especially those who are sober, talked about the efforts, particularly by the newcomers, to live up to the hard-drinking stereotype learned from their fathers and their fathers before them. As one sandhog stated, "It's basically a stereotype. I learned it from my father and he learned it from his." A third-gener-ation, Irish-American sandhog commented, "Growing up, I heard all these stories from him [points to his father]. So the drinking was no big deal to me and my friends. That is just the way it was."

The sandhogs recognized that their hard drinking behavior set them apart from other work groups. One member characterized the sandhogs as having "an immigrant Irish mentality that hasn't changed in a hundred years."

We were working for [Andrews Construction]. They're used to working with well-disciplined unions on their projects, mostly Italian immigrant laborers. And they do as they are told. The first four months, we caused pure hell for [Andrews] because they were unaccustomed to working with gangs of alcoholics. The company would tell the steward to kick so and so off the job because he was drunk. The steward would tell the company to go fuck themselves. The job was getting done. What was their beef? Finally, they gave up and let us do the job.

While distinguishing the sandhogs from other workers, drinking and its accompanying sense of marginality also helped ensure the continuity of their communal life. It ensured that other groups would not compete for these "disreputable" jobs and that the sandhogs could preserve those jobs for themselves and their children. Older sandhogs spoke about childhoods in which their parents underscored the inevitability of becoming a sandhog and closing off other options. One sandhog succinctly characterized these experiences:

Growing up [during the thirties and forties] all you knew was sandhogs. The kids you played with and went to school with were kids of sandhogs. All you knew about being a man was being a sandhog. You lived with the drinking and figured it was part of the work, part of the price you paid for being a sandhog. All you knew about being a parent was from your father drunk and your mother getting hit. Your parents always expected you to be a sandhog. If you thought about anything else, they said you weren't any better than anybody else on the block and that the work was good honest work, and having a job was all that mattered. Don't look for anything better. Accept what you've got. You weren't supposed to look at other options.

One union member, who grew up across from the bar where his father recruited gang members, spoke of the inevitability many felt about becoming a sandhog.

The banging on the bar and the fights that went on there. I was petrified. I thought I would never go near anybody who was a

sandhog; let alone working for them. . . . Economics decided alot
of our lives. And it decided mine. I know the first time I went
into a tunnel and they set off a blast of about 200 sticks of pow-
der, I said, "What in the name of God brought me to this place?"
That was my reaction. . . . When I went home, I had young children and I had to come back. (quoted in Collison 1994)

Similarly, a second-generation sandhog, who joined the union in the
late forties, commented,

My father was a sandhog. I had all my uncles and cousins in
[sandhogging]. . . . More or less I quit school. My father said,
"You aren't going to hang out on no corner. You either go to
school or work." That was the option. Then he took me for the
summer down in the hole. Out in Flatbush. A small little tunnel.
I took a liking to it. That was it. . . . At eighteen, I drank a few. On
the Lincoln Tunnel [roadway under the Hudson River], I drank
more. Pretty soon, I was drinking a quart a day.

Drinking and the Gangs

Gangs and drinking are a prevalent way of life in all mining, but in
the sandhog community, they are also related to the hiring practices
of the mid-nineteenth and early twentieth centuries. During this period, the saloons were both hiring halls and the hub of political organizing, and saloonkeepers were often politicians who had
parlayed their street gang and social club activities into powerful
political machines (Stivers 1985). In return for drink and work, gang
members voted for the boss; the street gang and machine club,
which centered on saloon life, were entwined.

At the time of the building of the Brooklyn Bridge, all hiring was
done out of the saloons, and one could not get on a work gang unless one drank and was a member of the saloon gang. Until recently,
the bars continued to function as hiring halls because, as one member put it, "foremen hire those guys they drink with." Consequently,
the sandhogs believed that they must drink in order to fit in. As one
old timer commented, "The attitude was you had to be a drinker. If

I didn't drink, I didn't get any work. . . . My attitude was drinking came with the job."

Although drinking was required for membership in the gang, it is important to recognize that, even before the culture started to be transformed, not all sandhogs drank intemperately. As one sandhog put it, "No one ever forced you to drink. You could drink or not drink in the tunnels. The thing was you didn't stop other guys from drinking or tell the boss." Many chose not to drink in the tunnels because they were too scared. Some sandhogs were and are regarded as social drinkers, who "have a few with the gang and go home." Others are "heavy hitters," who consume large quantities of alcohol with their work mates on and off the job. But, as one sandhog stated, "Generally, you drink with and hang out with those who drink like you."

Historically, when work was plentiful and extra men were needed for tunneling, the easy camaraderie of tavern drinking made the bars an ideal setting for recruitment of new gang members. One sandhog recounted how, as a newcomer in the seventies, when work was plentiful, he was recruited into sandhogging:

> When [the foreman] asked me, I was drinking in a bar. He says, "What are you doing? Do you want to be a sandhog?" I didn't know what a sandhog was. He said, "Be a sandhog like me and earn $500, $600 a week." I looked at him. Where is this $500, $600 a week? He just borrowed $20 off of me. I was only making $52 a week as a messenger. . . . I paid my $68 for membership dues. . . . Five weeks [later] . . . I took the train to Delancy Street and got hired on the second shift.

During the early seventies, many gangs from the Highbridge job in upper Manhattan recruited men from the bars.

> Everyone went to the bars [on that job]. In the morning, we would be missing two or three guys on the gang. So, we'd say, "Go up to the bars and see if anyone wants to work, regardless of whether they had a book [union card] or not." That's how some of those guys got in. We drank in those bars, so we knew them socially. So, we'd say, "Hey, you want to go to work?"

Shapers, union members looking for work, also visited the bars in hopes of getting on a gang. Here, they could listen in on the gossip network about which gangs were hiring and who was working where. If they were unable to get on a gang, they would often hang out at the bar drinking with and observing gang members who had just completed their shift.

First sandhog: When I was shaping, I'd go to a bar. I'd watch who was drinking and then I would have a pretty good idea who wasn't coming back the next day. Or who ain't going to make the second shift.

Second sandhog: Sometimes it was easier to go buy a guy a few drinks and take his job."

First sandhog: Yeah, I'd see who was hitting them heavy at lunchtime. I'd have a general idea who wasn't gonna make it back. Then I'd go to the hog house. When they asked where [Pete] was, I'd say, "I don't know."

Until the late seventies, drinking in the tunnels was still considered to be normal behavior by the sandhogs. Traditionally, "something in the boot" was part of every miners' outfit and on every gang "one guy always carried a big bag; he was the beer tender." During shape up, for instance, the foreman would often ask, "Who has something on the hip? Ok, you are on and don't go too far from me either." Gang members working in compressed air customarily opened or "cracked" their bottles before entering the tunnels in order to prevent them from exploding; when someone forgot to crack their bottle, the explosions were met with knowing laughter. Although the sandhogs assumed that everyone drank, they did not expect everyone to drink in the tunnels. Rather, "it was your choice. You were of your own mind. If you wanted to drink it was OK." As one sandhog observed, "Twenty years ago, you still had big gangs. Thirty, forty guys in a gang. I'd say at least half was always drinking in the tunnel. We'd bring down cases of beer. There was one guy on the jumbo who just kept the beer coming. That was his job." Another commented: "It was an amazing thing to see. . . . You could drink all you wanted, and get as drunk as you wanted but keep drilling, keep loading dynamite. But I never saw any of them set off, or hook the wrong wire up. It was an expected part of the job. You drank and you got drunk. As long as you could do your work it was OK."

In the tunnels, gang members often went to great lengths to protect their supply of alcohol. The priority put upon drinking and ensuring a plentiful supply is clearly revealed by the following account:

> [Bobby] was a beer drinker. He could drink two cases a day. . . . We had to put these big lights in the shaft. . . . We loaded up the top of the cage [an elevator] with forty lights. . . . He asked, "You got everything?" I had to buy him a bottle of whiskey and two cases of beer for the afternoon. There was no room on the cage so I brought the whiskey with me. We go all the way to the top and he says, "Give me one of my beers." Gee, I left them down the bottom. He says, "Take the cage back down, take them lights off the cage, and put my beer on." Priorities!

When working in compressed air, the sandhogs work for three hours and then go up top to decompress for three hours. During this period, they would customarily drink in either the hog house or a tavern. As one old-timer explained, these "three hours were the ruin of the sandhogs. You'd come out of the hole and have three hours to hang out before you went back down. So where did you go? To the bar. Or go to sleep on top of the locker. That was your choice. So you go and have a couple and in three hours you get a nice load on. You go back down and in three minutes you'd be sober."

Contractors were ambivalent about the drinking. They would sometimes try to discipline gang members for drinking and found that they could not do so. As one sandhog observed, "Everyone came back from those three hours tanked up. You didn't dare, no matter who you were as a boss, fuck around with union conditions because you'd have eight, nine guys on your ass. Shop stewards, everyone was drinking. Everyone was ready for bear. You fuck around [with the drinking] and everyone was all over you like shit on a fly." Consequently, contractors ended up making the best of the situation by rewarding the men with liquor and beer for a job well done.

> I worked on jobs where supervision sent in three, four bottles every day. . . . If we made five rings, they came up with three

bottles of booze for our shaft gang. I said, "Some of us drink beer," and they said, "OK, two bottles and two cases of beer."

When I was in the tunnels in 1985, union rules prohibited drinking in the tunnels. Although I did not witness any men drinking in the tunnels at that time, my informants told me that some of the men occasionally drank on the job. An AA member recounted how, on his Sunday morning shift, a gang showed up with a thermos of Bloody Marys, a bottle of Johnny Walker Black, and a couple of cases of Heinekin. Later, they went out for more. While they were gone the AA member locked up the tools because he "wasn't taking any more chances with that bunch of drunks." Similarly, "holing through," which is the completion of a tunnel, was still being celebrated with impromptu drinking parties. For instance, one sandhog stated, "The day we holed through, connecting the Central Park and Highbridge sections of the Water Tunnel Number 3, everyone was drinking on the job. Hell! It's always been part of the job." Even *The New York Times* noted the impromptu holing-through celebrations 600 feet below Columbia University with its 1985 front-page photo captioned, "A Great Day for Sandhogs!" The accompanying story, documenting the jubilant mood of the miners, noted their "hooting and hollering, grinning and punching one another on the shoulders" (Geist 1985). It failed to note however, their celebratory drinking.

Although the union prohibits drinking in the tunnels, it still permits members to drink in the hog house. Indeed, the sandhogs have always drunk in the hog houses, frequently turning the soda machines into beer machines and customarily loading the refrigerator with cases of beer. On the Lincoln Tunnel in the fifties, for instance, they turned the hog house into a restaurant complete with bar.

This guy started with a frankfurter cart outside the gate. . . .
There were three, four hundred men on that job. He wanted to
make a restaurant so they made a place for him in the hog
house. It was more booze he sold than anything else. Thirty-five
cents a shot. Night and day. That went on for four years. Then he
retired and went to Florida.

In 1985, whenever I visited the hog houses at Van Cortland Park, Roosevelt Island, and Highbridge—all part of Water Tunnel Number

3—whether it was 6:00 A.M., noon, 6:00 P.M., or midnight, the sand-hogs were enjoying themselves by joking, telling stories, ribbing one another, recounting the events of jobs past, and sometimes quarrel-ing. Within this context, it was not unusual to see some men drink-ing. One morning when I went to shape up at Van Cortland Park, several men were already seated at a table drinking beer with their breakfast sandwiches—fried eggs on a hard roll. Nearby, several oth-ers were playing poker and drinking beer. On this same morning, one of my companions pointed to a fellow who had spent the night sleeping on one of the benches because he had been too drunk to go home. Later that day, we visited another hog house at Highbridge and found that the miners were venting the fumes out of the tunnel through the main shaft. Many of the sandhogs who had been forced from their work by the thick, gray, acrid smoke were clearing their throats with a cold Budweiser. At lunchtime, groups of sandhogs sat in the hog house drinking beer and swapping tall tales. Several days later, I visited Roosevelt Island, from approximately 9 P.M. until 2 A.M., and once again witnessed such drinking. After each shift, gangs would congregate in the hog houses to drink and recount the day's events before heading home or to a tavern. Those guys who couldn't get on a gang often hung out at the hog house all day long, pooling their money to buy a bottle of whiskey and a twelve-pack of beer. These incidents were clearly visible to everyone, and there was no attempt made to conceal such drinking. Drinking in the hog house was regarded as normal.

Traditionally, after work, gang members expected their work mates to go to the bars and drink with them. In the ethnic commu-nities of the nineteenth century, saloons were the workingman's so-cial club, where craftsmen as well as laborers went to pass the time with their friends (Rosenzweig 1983). Likewise, in the early days of sandhogging, gang members were expected to return to their neigh-borhoods and drink with their work mates. Today, the old neigh-borhoods are no longer intact. They began disappearing in the sixties. In the seventies and eighties, however, most of the gangs still expected their members to go to a bar after work, where they re-counted the day's exploits and washed away the pain and horrors of the tunnel.

In the bars, the sandhogs made new workers feel a part of the gang for the first time. One member remembers how, as a newcomer, after a difficult first day in the tunnel, the crew welcomed him: "I wanted out, man. I wanted to run. But after a while, you come up and go to a bar. Everybody talking; everybody patting me on the head; no one would take my money. So, I'm here now—a member of the crew." In the old days, the "social drinkers had their three, four beers [with the guys after work] and went home." Others drifted from one drinking group to another; some of these people did not go home for days and ended up drinking with whomever was available.

Twenty years ago, in Van Cortland Park and on Roosevelt Island, . . . a lot of those guys never went home. They were living in the hog house, wives coming to the hog houses looking for pay checks, guys hadn't been home in two weeks. . . . [Bill's] whole gang would leave the job, go to the bar, leave the bar and go to the Park, leave the Park and go to work. Sometimes, they'd go two, three days in a row.

Drinking with gang members on and off the job was regarded by the sandhog community as normal behavior, an expected part of the job. One drank in order to become a member of the gang, and then one drank with one's gang members. Gangs drank together in the tunnels, the hog houses, and in the bars, melding their work and leisure activities. Such drinking was tolerated by both the union and the contractors well into the seventies; consequently, the sandhogs believed that "if you wanted to work, you drank." Drinking was part of the job; it was the cultural glue, bonding gang members to one another.

Drinking and Work-Related Emotions

Ceremonial drinking, in addition to constructing communal boundaries, enhances group solidarity (Douglas 1987). Historically, sandhog drinking increased the bonding among gang members because, as a ritual, it reinforced the work-related emotions shared by the sandhogs in their communal lives. Drinking occasions highlighted the sandhogs' shared sense of danger, pride of craftsmanship, and playfulness. When gang members drank together, these work-related emotions were brought into sharp relief, underscoring the common life shared by members. Consequently, the sandhogs traditionally experienced drinking with one another as emotionally engaging and rewarding.

In particular, gang drinking highlighted the danger shared by members. In both primitive and complex societies, drinking is a culturally prescribed technique for reducing anxiety and stress (e.g., Horton 1945; Field 1962; Bales 1946; Bacon 1945; Linsky, Colby, and Straus 1991); similarly, many occupations prescribe drinking as a means of of coping with unpleasant working conditions (Martin, Blum, and Roman 1992). Likewise, sandhog drinking is a culturally prescribed technique for coping with the stress of dangerous working conditions within the tunnels. Within the context of the gangs, the sandhogs learned to manage their fears by drinking. Consequently, they used to claim that one had to be "either drunk or crazy to work in the tunnels."

According to the sandhogs, their fears occur because there is no formal apprenticeship program; rather, they learn tunneling by shaping one job after another. Consequently, they are "prone to operating out of fear and managing it by drinking." As one sandhog observed,

> The fear is overwhelming. . . . You didn't know what you were doing. I didn't know how to "scale"—to follow the fucking vein. I remember one time. I was scaling and the whole thing came down. I had two choices: Run or be buried alive. . . . I could feel the shit as it came down. I didn't understand how it came down and it ate up the back of my rubber boots. . . . I was scared. . . . After I got out of the hole, I went right to the bar.

Another sandhog told me, "A lot of the time, I was afraid. I'd drink. The difference is when you work in an office you have got to be sharp. With us, we could drink and get away with it." Another adds, "I was afraid but so was everyone else. The boss was yelling at me and I realized he was yelling out of fear too."

Although drinking on the job was culturally prescribed, this does not mean that the sandhogs drank in an unrestrained manner. Rather, they drank to relieve their fears but did so in a manner which would not endanger the gang. This norm is reflected by one sandhog who described attempting to hide his developing alco-holism from the rest of the gang. "I was so self-conscious of every-thing I did [when I was drinking]. If I was sober and slipped, I didn't give a fuck, but when I was hung over. . . . I didn't want any-body looking. Paranoia! You know every mistake you make, even if it is a stupid mistake, they are going to be looking at you." Another added, "I wouldn't drink in the tunnels. I couldn't drink and work because I got sloppy. I'd drink and fall down. I didn't want to make any mistakes down there."

The following account suggests how the sandhogs' camaraderie in gang drinking helped dispel their fear.

> As soon as I got out of the hole, I went to the bar. Drinking! Shaking! Scared! I laughed it off. That happened on many occa-sions. Sometimes, out of stupidity I would put my fingers in be-tween the steel to see if the hole matched up with the bolt. Or, sometimes they would be shoving the steel together, I would not be looking, and it would take my glove off. . . . I would go to the bar and drink and laugh about it. Fucking joke!

According to another, "After the shift, you would want to get para-lyzed." One old-timer recounted that, after a shift in compressed air, the gang would race out of the decompression chamber, hop into their cars, and speed at eighty miles an hour to the bars.

Drinking also highlighted the pride the sandhogs take in their work. Wherever sandhogs gather they talk about their work, but drinking always brings out such boastfulness. Members talked in-cessantly about their current projects and about jobs of yesterday as though they were still happening. They boasted about the crafts-manship of their work and recounted stories about the obstacles overcome to make it right. Past drinking practices enhanced their sense of craftsmanship and the pride they felt in their sweat labor.

In their boastful talk, they were particularly proud that the drink-ing never affected their craftmanship. One sandhog proudly pro-claimed: "The work was always done. We never failed on any job. A bent thing here and there or a beer can embedded in the cement when they pulled the form off. But the work always got done. We never missed a tunnel by that much. We didn't put a piece of steel in where it shouldn't be or any dumb-ass thing."

Additionally, the sandhogs boastfully claimed that their drinking caused few serious accidents; rather, they attributed the majority of the accidents to either stupidity or sloppiness: a lack of craftsmanship.

> We lost a lot of men at Highbridge. [No more than] two of them, I can't swear to it, had anything to do with drinking. Bad judgment and just accidents. Being in the wrong place at the wrong time. I don't remember ever seeing anybody ever get killed or hurt real bad where I could say if the fucker were sober it wouldn't have happened. . . . Once in a while, you would get a guy who was either hung over or didn't think too right. Just did something real stupid down there and didn't give a fuck.

Another quickly added that no union would admit that accidents happen because of drinking. "If they admit two out of a hundred being due to alcohol, it's probably sixty. But no one really knows. . . . When [Sammy] fell down drunk and cracked his head, the story that came out was he got beat up in a bar so his family could get the insurance."

Drinking also soothed the sandhogs' injured pride when they felt that their work was unappreciated. According to one sandhog, "Embarrassment plays a big role in the drinking. One moment you have a big fucking ego because you did a great job. The next, you got low self-esteem." Another added, "When you worked with some of the foremen I worked with, you wanted to drink. I worked with a couple of prick bosses. [He would shout] 'pick up that pipe, you fucking weak bastard!' It hurts your pride first of all and you want to hit him with the pipe. . . . After a day with him, you had so much anger you wanted to kill this prick. I would drink instead."

Drinking rituals also highlighted the sandhogs' sense of playfulness. Drinking occasions, especially those above ground, are always playful because they are accompanied by a great deal of horsing around, storytelling, betting, arm wrestling, and mock battles. Sometimes drinking results in fist fights, which the sandhogs appear to regard as fun. Indeed, some sandhogs are known for their fighting abilities, and their exploits are retold endlessly within the community. Drinking was also playful in the sense that it symbolized the transition from the high state of alert necessary in the tunnels to the relaxed relationships above ground. Emotions kept in check in the tunnel were allowed to enter group life within the relative safety of the hog house and tavern.

Drinking, then, highlighted the work-related emotions shared by the sandhogs and increased the communal bonding among gang members because it was emotionally engaging and rewarding. Drinking occasions permitted the sandhogs to joke about the day's close calls and release their pent-up fears. In doing so, the sandhogs underscored the obligations members owed to one another: eternal vigilance guaranteed a safe passage into and out of the tunnels. At the same time, drinking celebrated their safe passage and highlighted the day's accomplishments: a job well done.

Drinking, Occupational Morality, and Self

The occupational morality that emerged from the sandhogs' drinking rituals was focused upon preserving the communal life; they communicated to gang members the community's basic assumptions. While drinking rituals strengthened their communal bonds with one another, the rituals did so by underscoring the individual sandhog's primary obligation to preserve the group by protecting his fellow drinkers. His duties were to ensure their employability and safety within the tunnels above all else. Encapsulated within the symbolic boundary of drinking, the sandhog looked inward to his occupational community, paying little attention to the society beyond. Indeed, the outside world was experienced as hostile to his way of life.

Drinking reinforced group solidarity because it symbolized the obligations members owed to one another. Recruitment into the gangs was dependent on one's drinking relationships: the foremen hired those with whom they drank, and the gang was made up of men who drank together. As one sandhog explains, "Everybody you knew drank. . . . We narrowed it down to drinkers. If you didn't drink, I didn't trust you. I didn't want to know you."

The obligation to hire those with whom one drinks is highlighted by a story told by one sandhog who tried to stop drinking and sober up. He was "blackballed from the gang," with which he had been shaping for three months.

[The gang leader's] father was a walking boss on the job. He [the father] was dying of alcoholism. He had a resentment that I stopped drinking. . . . I was getting ready to change my clothes. I was shaping and he [the gang leader] walked right by me. I said, "What is the story?" He said, "The old man said I can't take you down anymore." He mumbled some shit and said, "Look, I can't go against my father."

When the sandhog quit drinking, he became untrustworthy and the obligation to hire him on the gang disappeared.

Although trust was symbolized by drinking, it was also predicated upon one's drinking group. For instance, "New York" (i.e., Manhattan) gangs felt obligated to hire New Yorkers with whom they drank and the Donkeys, Irish sandhogs from Brooklyn, felt obligated to hire Donkeys. As one sandhog observed: "The Donkeys were very particular who they took down. They wouldn't take down any drunken New Yorkers. They drank too but they would rather take down a guy off the fucking street." The experience of one recovering New Yorker who shaped a Donkey gang, shortly after he first tried to sober up, further highlights the relationship between drinking and trust: "I was going from working with a bunch of guys I trusted to working with a bunch of crazy Irishmen over there. It was insanity. They took me every day. I hated it because I didn't know anybody. They were a different breed."

Drinking became one's admission ticket to the gang, and one was obligated to supply the gang with alcohol. The priority that the sandhogs put upon the obligation to preserve their supply of alcohol is brought to light by a story told by a beer tender.

I had them [the cases of beer] in suitcases. . . . I was driving to work one day and the fucking car started blowing up. . . . A cab pulled over and asked, "Can I help you?" I said, "Yeah!" and started to load the beer into the cab. He asked, "What you doing?" I said, "I gotta get to work. Fuck the car! This is what keeps me working. As long as I feed these animals, I stay working." I left the car there for three days. . . . The tires were gone, the battery was gone, the front seats were gone. The important thing was you had to be there [in the tunnel with the beer].

In the tunnels, gang members are obligated, because of the ever present danger, to watch out for one another; drinking, however, highlighted this obligation. According to one sandhog, watching out for one another is "normal; you've got friends down there you drink with, hang out with. Then, you've got to really make sure."

Also recall that the sandhogs never fire anyone; gang members protect one another's job, only refusing to recruit individuals who have proven to be lazy or to have done something so stupid that it endangered the gang. These obligations were underscored, when, in the opinion of gang members, someone had drunk too much and may endanger themselves or the rest of the gang. "That is part of sandhogging. If you are that drunk, the boss will tell you to go home. . . . If you do your work, and it don't happen all of the time, the majority of the bosses will pay you for the day." Alternatively, the foreman might give the sandhog light-duty work where he will not endanger himself or the gang. One sandhog recalled coming to work right from the bar and being so drunk that he could not walk a straight line. The gang leader made him the hog house man for the day. In the tunnels, "if they saw you were drinking too much, they said, 'Go sit over there.' "

Gang members customarily carried those who drank too much to adjacent tunnels, where they could sleep it off safe from harm and without endangering the rest the gang. "The majority of the sandhogs, if you're screwed up, will take care of you. They'll put you in a room. But, don't do it all the time. One day, down the line, you'll go into that room before the job is over. As long as you don't cause no trouble, they'll take care of you." When the sandhog returned from that "room," however, he felt obliged to "work twice as hard to make up for the missed day."

Generally, bosses and gang members were very tolerant of drunkenness, ejecting someone from the tunnels only when he became "real loud and boisterous" and was "really out of line."

We were working in Brooklyn in the middle of a shaft. There was a hole with boards over it. . . . Fucking [Bill] comes along drunk. He was staggering and falling. We were afraid he would fall in. We waited for [the gang leader] to say something. [Bill] could fall down the hole. Finally, he said, "Look, go upstairs and sleep it off."

As in other occupations (e.g., Mars 1987), the sandhogs' drinking rituals set up powerful exchange relationships. A foreman became the recipient of drinks bought by gang members with the expectation that he would hire them on his gangs. Within the gangs, there were also drinking rules about reciprocity; customarily, members bought one another rounds of drinks and everyone with money was expected to participate. These drinking practices are similar to those in other mining communities (e.g., Dennis, Henriques, and Slaughter 1969; Douglas and Isherwood 1980); and they ensure that those who drink regularly with one another will be employed on the gangs. Sandhog drinking symbolized one's obligations to ensure employment for one's drinking companions.

Although some members may have drunk for the physical effects of alcohol, the essential points are that they drank communally and the drinking rituals underscored the duties they owed to one another. Before tackling a particularly difficult task, drinking served as a time out. Gang members would share a drink which symbolically drew their attention to the presence of the group and the watchfulness they owed to one another in the present enterprise. Likewise, drinking afterwards came to symbolize that the group had survived the ordeal. When tragedy occurred, heavy drinking was de rigueur. It deadened the pain and renewed the obligation that the survivors owed to one another: eternal vigilance. Such occasions were punctuated with stories of heroism in the face of danger or the mundane things that members have done to protect one another's back. One sandhog recounted the tale of Smiley, who had risked his life to hold up the tunnel so that the other gang members could escape. Such stories when accompanied with drink underscored the ever-present danger faced in the tunnels and the sacrifices that gang members make for one another.

Not surprisingly, drinking provided the sandhogs with a valued self-image. As they stated repeatedly, sandhogs drank because life in the gangs required them to be drinkers. If one did not drink, one did not fit in: "If you were a straight arrow, no one wanted anything to do with you down there." Nondrinkers were outsiders who could not be trusted to ensure one's employability or safety in the tunnels.

The requirement to drink, however, did not mean that all sandhogs were alcoholics or that they all had drinking problems. They respected the sandhog who knew how to hold his liquor, and they continue to make distinctions between "social" and "problem" drinkers. Social drinkers have their "three or four beers and go home," and problem drinkers repeatedly consume so much alcohol that they endanger themselves and the rest of the gang. The essential sandhog self, however, was built around being a drinker, and those do-gooders who attempted to take alcohol away from a sandhog were greeted with anger and scorn because they did not understand what it meant to be a miner.

The Persistence of Sandhog Drinking

How does one explain the persistence of the sandhog intemperate drinking culture in a world hostile to drinking on the job? The data suggest that its explanation is primarily cultural; its persistence for more than one hundred years lies in the special meaning that the sandhogs attached to drinking alcohol.

From a cultural perspective, drinking marked the sandhogs' communal boundaries, separating them from outsiders and underscoring what they had in common and the obligations owed to one another. It also supplied them with a valued self-image, the two-fisted, hard-drinking craftsman who confronts dangers unknown to the rest of the world. Drinking took on its distinctive meaning in relation to the centrality of the gang in work and social life. The gang remains the keystone of a sandhog's survival, representing both his economic security and a slender life line against sudden death. Drinking symbolized the common life they shared, emphasizing its danger, their pride of craft, and their playfulness. At the same time, it highlighted their obligations to ensure one another's employment and safety. When the sandhogs drank together they symbolically reconstructed their community. Drinking rituals, then, reinforced group solidarity, and the more often they were performed the stronger were the bonds uniting members.

These cultural meanings were passed on from generation to generation as fathers recruited sons into the union. Like other construction trades (Riemer 1979), fathers gave sons first preference for work, generally recruiting them when they were still in high school by finding them summer employment on one of the gangs. Of course, not all of these sons returned after completing their education, but many of them did. The rest drifted into other lines of work, often in one of the other construction trades and sometimes in a professional occupation.

The sandhogs' intemperate drinking culture was also passed on to men whose families had not been members of the occupation. Often, these men were recruited by gang leaders in bars during periods of full employment. Once on a gang, they, like the sandhogs' sons, learned that drinking on the job was regarded as acceptable behavior and that gang members were expected to drink with one another after leaving the tunnels as well. They learned the justifications for drinking in the tunnels (e.g., to cope with dangerous conditions), their responsibilities for taking care of those who drank too much (e.g., covering up and laying them out in adjacent tunnels to sober up). In addition, they experienced drinking as a means of distinguishing themselves from other workers and strenghtening the communal bonds among themselves.

The acceptability of drinking in the tunnels was further reinforced by the contractors' behavior. Like the managers in a gypsum mine studied by Gouldner (1954), they appeared to accept the sandhogs' intemperate drinking because they felt that they had little choice and believed that the miners function in a world of their own. The contractors accepted the inevitability of drinking and encouraged it by rewarding good performance with liquor and beer. The sandhogs' intemperate drinking culture was taken for granted among the contractors as well as the sandhogs.

The persistence of intemperate drinking cultures within some occupational communities may be explained by the meanings which members attach to drinking: that is, they experience their intemperate drinking rituals as the means for constructing and reconstructing their sense of community. Drinking rituals solidify occupational boundaries by enhancing members' sense of self and underscoring the obligations they owe one another; thus, they promote communal bonding among members. If changes in occupational drinking behavior are to occur, the meanings that workers attach to their intemperate drinking must be transformed.

5 *Transforming the Sandhog Drinking Culture*

While supporting the occupational community's basic assumptions, the sandhogs' intemperate drinking rituals provided an ideal environment for the development of alcohol problems. On the one hand, drinking symbolized the obligations members owed to one another and reinforced their communal bonding; on the other, the easy camaraderie of the bars and hog houses encouraged even the social drinkers to occasionally consume too much alcohol before driving home. These settings provided those drinkers who might have been predisposed toward alcoholism with an excellent cover for their developing drinking problems. Given these conditions, how did a temperate drinking culture become established and become taken for granted within the sandhogs?

In order for cultural transformation to occur, drinking rituals must be reframed as destroying, rather than strengthening, communal bonds, and this reframing must be continually reinforced until the new beliefs are taken for granted. Within the sandhogs, this reframing occurred when its labor market collapsed and a community member successfully reframed the problem of unemployment within the context of the alcoholism movement. Specifically, he argued that those unemployed sandhogs unable to find alternative work suffered from alcoholism and required treatment for their illnesses, and that the union had a fraternal obligation to provide such assistance. Building its alcoholism program on the beliefs of Alcoholics Anonymous, the occupational community transformed its intemperate drinking culture by teaching alcoholic members that they did not need to drink in order to be sandhogs. The union emphasized that the program's helping ethic was the real basis of strong communal bonds. In this process, the sandhogs created a new communal identity of themselves in which intemperate drinking is no longer emotionally rewarding and does not define membership in the community. The sandhogs continue to construct their sense of community symbolically, but today their consciousness of kind is based upon the naturally occurring rituals of their shared work experiences and their communal commitment to helping one another in difficult times.

The Alcoholics Anonymous Program

Alcoholics Anonymous has had a major impact upon Americans' perceptions of drinking problems, and its philosophy underlies the modern treatment of alcoholism both in the workplace and in the larger community.[1] It is necessary to understand the philosophy of AA and the processes by which it transforms its members' sense of self in order to comprehend how the sandhogs have used it to transform their intemperate drinking culture. The AA transformation of self entails redefining the individual's relationship to alcohol so that he or she comes to see him or herself as nothing but an alcoholic and comes to realize that his or her only salvation lies in living by AA's twelve-step program (Rudy 1986; Denzin 1987a, 1987b). The trans-

---

[1] Although generally well thought of within the professional treatment community, AA is not always well understood by either social scientists or treatment personnel (Leach and Norris 1977; Trice and Staudenmeier 1989; Miller and Kurtz 1994). In part, this is because there have been few rigorous studies comparing it with other interventions (e.g., National Institute of Medicine, 1990; Walsh et al. 1992). This misunderstanding may also exist because AA's techniques appear to Americans to be too heavily couched in religious beliefs for our aggressively secular time. For instance, rational emotive psychotherapists complain that AA imprisons individuals within the group rather than teaching them to be emotionally free agents who act rationally (Hall 1990; Ellis and Schoenfeld 1990; Ellis and Velten 1992; Trimpey 1989).

formation experienced by AA members is well documented in the social science literature (e.g., Maxwell 1984; Rudy 1986; Denzin 1987a, 1987b). Here I sketch the outlines of the AA program so that we can see it at work within the sandhog community.

From the fortuitous meeting of two alcoholics in 1935, AA had by 1990 grown into a worldwide organization of 1,793,834 members in 87,696 groups in 136 countries (Alcoholics Anonymous 1990).[2] AA changes the individual's symbolic relationship to alcohol by situating him or her at the center of a life and death drama (Antze 1987; Denzin 1987a, 1987b; Ford 1989). In this drama, the individual struggles with alcohol, discovers that he cannot escape from this subtle foe, and finally, after hitting bottom, experiences a spiritual reawakening by surrendering to a "Higher Power" and religiously following AA's twelve-step program for living a sober life.[3] This drama is an individual rite of passage in which the individual is transformed from a disreputable drunk into a respectable citizen who is called to help other suffering alcoholics (Sonnenstuhl 1990; Antze 1987).

In the separation stage of this rite, the individual discovers that he or she is an alcoholic and must quit drinking in order to live. As the drama unfolds, the sufferer learns that he or she has a disease caused by a physical sensitivity to, and mental obsession with, alcohol. *Physical sensitivity* refers to the inability of the alcoholic to control the amount of alcohol he or she consumes. AAs regard physical sensitivity as irreversible and often describe it as an allergy. Consequently, when the alcoholic picks up that first drink, he or she is condemned to drink well past the point of intoxication. "Mental obsession" refers to some unknown force that condemns the alcoholic to take that first drink anyway. These two ideas place the alcoholic

---

[2] It is difficult to know exactly how many people actually count themselves as members of AA. AA collects its data anonymously from members who happen to be attending a particular AA meeting. Because many participants do not attend meetings regularly and are not present when these data are collected, they are not counted in AA's statistics.

[3] Many observers have commented upon AA's relationship to traditional religious forms (e.g., Antze 1987) and argued about whether AA is itself a religion (Gellman 1964; Jones 1970; Whitley 1977; Kurtz 1979). AA, however, emphatically insists that it is not a religion even though its central teaching is that alcoholics can only recover with help from a power greater than themselves and even though it relies heavily upon many of the trappings of traditional religions: confessions, testimonials, prayers, and regular missions to the unconverted.

in a classic double bind (Bateson 1971): the person cannot drink because it will kill him or her but also lacks the power to stop drinking. When the alcoholic recognizes this bind, he or she experiences utter hopelessness and despair and becomes willing to surrender to AA's message.

At this point in the drama, the alcoholic enters the liminal or transformation stage in which he or she is neither the old or new self because he or she no longer knows how to behave. In this stage, the newcomer to AA learns to be repentant, admitting to powerlessness over alcohol and opening himself or herself to a spiritual awakening by turning personal will over to a Higher Power. AAs are free to conceive of this Higher Power as they wish, but they tend to describe it as a warm supportive figure providing strength and courage in hours of need (Antze 1987). It is never described as a judging deity; rather, members describe the Higher Power, like AA itself, as essentially playing an accepting and comforting role in moments of crisis.

According to AA, the alcoholic's lack of defense against drinking lies in a spiritual condition, a deep-seated attitude toward life that is self-centered: "Selfishness—self-centeredness! That, we think, is at the root of our troubles. . . . The alcoholic is an extreme example of self-will run riot, though he usually doesn't think so. Above everything, we alcoholics must be rid of this selfishness. We must or it kills us!" (AA 1955: 62).

Through the twelve steps, alcoholics are transformed; they are released from their selfishness and experience a spiritual awakening. According to AA, this transformation requires the Higher Power's help in the removal of the alcoholic's "character defects"—the dangerous emotional habits that stem from selfishness—and involves him or her in a strenuous ethical regimen of confession, repentance, and restitution in order to purge this self-centeredness. Following the twelve steps, each individual makes a searching and fearless inventory of himself or herself, admits shortcomings to the Higher Power, and makes amends to whomever he or she has harmed. This repentant role is particularly evident in the comeback stories AAs tell about their hedonistic lives with alcohol and how the program saved them (Trice and Roman 1970a; Ford 1989).

Finally, in the incorporation stage, each individual is incorporated into the calling or helping role: The alcoholic demonstrates his or her selfless attitude by doing twelfth-step work, which means carrying the message of sobriety to suffering alcoholics.[4] Twelfth-stepping is therapeutic and insures AA members against slipping into old emotional habits that will inevitably lead to drinking (Rudy 1986; Denzin 1987a, 1987b). According to *Alcoholics Anonymous*, which members call the "Big Book" (AA 1955: 89), "Practical experience shows that nothing will so much ensure immunity from drinking as work with other alcoholics. It works when other activities fail." The alcoholism program by which the sandhogs are transforming their intemperate culture builds upon AA's helping role.

Unfreezing the Intemperate Drinking Culture

In the mid-seventies, after nearly a hundred years of constructing their communal life around alcohol, the sandhogs began transforming their intemperate drinking culture into a temperate one. The mechanism for this change was the development of their alcoholism program, which is based upon their understanding of AA's beliefs and practices: alcoholism is a disease; alcoholics cannot drink; and the best way for alcoholics to remain sober is to help other alcoholics become and remain sober. In introducing these beliefs into the sandhog community, the program undermined the old belief that one had to drink in order to be a sandhog and the intemperate drinking rituals associated with that belief. Eventually drinking no longer marked the community's boundaries and was no longer able to create strong communal bonds among members. The program, like the nineteenth-century temperance union reforms, replaced the community's intemperate beliefs with a mutual aid ethic emphasizing that the community's survival depended upon members becoming sober and living respectable lives.[5]

[4] It is called "twelfth step work" because the twelfth step of AA's program states, "Having had a spiritual awakening as the result of these steps [the first eleven], we tried to carry this message to alcoholics and to practice these principles in all our affairs." AAs do this in order to maintain their own sobriety.

[5] Although there are strong parallels between workers' involvement in the Washingtonians, the Red and Blue Ribbon Reform Clubs, and AA, today's workers seem to be unaware of those earlier temperance reform programs and the vital role of workers in them. Indeed, few people, either inside or outside the labor movement, seem to realize that workers, as well as other Americans, were helping one another to live sober and respectable lives long before Bill W. and Dr. Bob established AA.

Environmental upheavals create opportunities for new beliefs to arise in an occupational community because they threaten the group's survival, making members, at least temporarily, uncertain about the obligations they owe to one another (Wuthnow 1987; Swindler 1986). During these upheavals, members may search for new ways of making sense of their problems and reconstructing their relationships to one another. Often, they experiment with beliefs imported from outside the community, which they later decide to adopt or reject. The unfreezing stage, then, is initiated by an upheaval within the occupational community's environment and concludes with a decision to adopt a new set of beliefs for making sense of the community's changed circumstances.

During their long history, the sandhogs experienced a number of layoffs that drove many tunnel workers into other lines of work. Although those instances presented the sandhogs with opportunities for transforming their intemperate drinking culture, no such change occurred. In the mid-seventies, they experienced another layoff. This time circumstances were different, and a set of temperate beliefs that would eventually transform their intemperate drinking culture into a temperate one were adopted within the community. The crucial difference was that, during this period, a leader who championed the belief that alcoholism was a disease rose within the union. He reframed the community's unemployment problems within this context and convinced the union to adopt an alcoholism program as a means of helping members to achieve sobriety and find work.

In the seventies, New York City experienced a severe fiscal crisis and canceled the construction of Water Tunnel Number 3. This was a serious threat to the sandhogs. They appeared to be destined for a permanent layoff and the complete dissolution of their occupational community. Initially, the sandhogs reacted to the layoff as they had in the past. Those members able to find work elsewhere left the union; these people were either younger workers or experienced sandhogs with other marketable skills. One sandhog recalled those days: "We lost a lot of good people back then. A lot of kids. They went into other trades. Some went to college. We lost them because we didn't have the work. It's too bad. Those kids would have been good for the union."

On an organizational level, the union reacted by taking political action, pressuring the city and state to reopen the tunnels and complete the project (Delaney 1983). After listening to the contractors and city officials bickering over funding, the sandhogs decided to take matters into their own hands by conducting a vigorous public relations campaign to alert the citizens of New York to the urgent need for the tunnel. They created a full-time public relations and political action position for a sandhog, who proved to be an able spokesman for the group in the city, as well as in the corridors of Albany and Washington. They addressed community and business groups and lobbied their city, state, and federal representatives, patiently explaining the dire consequences to New York City if Water Tunnel Number 3 were not completed before the old, existing water tunnels collapsed. They also produced several videos that were shown to many of these groups in an effort to educate them about the history of water in New York City generally and the necessity for completing Tunnel 3. When one of these videos, *City without Water*, was shown at a Chamber of Commerce meeting, the assembled officials, fearing an exodus of business and customers, pleaded with the sandhogs not to show it publicly. In return, the officials promised to put their formidable lobbying weight behind the sandhogs' efforts to procure new contracts for completion of the first stage of Water Tunnel Number 3.

Meanwhile, many sandhogs remained unemployed; these tended to be older men who had few employment options because they lacked alternative skills. Like many other unemployed blue-collar workers, many of these men spent their newly acquired leisure with their friends at the taverns because they had nothing else to do (LeMasters 1975; Ames and Janes 1987).[6] According to one sandhog: "These guys had nothing better to do. They couldn't get work anywhere and all they knew was sandhogging. So, they went to the bars every day, waiting for a job to open up. They weren't good for any-

[6] Data generally demonstrate a strong correlation between unemployment and alcohol problems (Brenner 1973, 1975; Barnes and Russell 1977; Ojesjo 1980; Jacobson and Lindsay 1980), and this may be particularly true for those men who belong to an occupational community with an intemperate drinking culture. For instance, Ames and Janes (1987) found that some workers reduced their consumption of alcohol after they were laid off because unemployment separates them from the support of their job-based drinking group and because they have family and social obligations to direct their energies away from drinking. In contrast, those unemployed workers who did not have such family and social obligations retained their involvement with the job-based drinking group and drank heavily.

thing else." In such cases, incipient alcohol problems held in check by daily employment routines can quickly go out of control, revealing the darker consequences of intemperate drinking cultures. In public testimony, the sandhogs' business agent, Richard Fitzsimmons, noted the shutdown's effects on his men:

> The tunnel workers are really hurting in this situation. These men have worked hard all their lives and now they're out in the streets with families to support. We are seeing more men with marital problems, more alcoholism, people losing their homes. We are a small union and we all know each other. It's terrible to see the toll this layoff is taking on the men and their families. (quoted in Delaney 1983: 52–55)

This unstable environment provided an opportunity for the introduction of new beliefs into the occupational community. This process requires a leader to champion the beliefs, especially when they call deeply embedded cultural practices into question (Deal and Kennedy 1982; Trice and Beyer 1991). In order for the champion's new message to be heard by community members, however, he or she must frame the new beliefs so that they are in alignment with existing cultural elements that need not change. Within this context, leaders in the employee assistance movement of the seventies argued that unions ought to adopt alcoholism programs because they had a fraternal obligation to help sick members, whether they suffered from cancer, heart disease, or alcoholism (Trice and Roman 1972; Johnson 1981).

Jimmy M., a well-respected sandhog who traces his lineage in the union back several generations, is the champion credited with importing into the union via his AA involvement the belief that alcoholism is a disease. In the seventies, there were apparently few sandhogs who were members of AA. They reckon their number at about half a dozen, and they were uncomfortable about revealing their AA involvement to other sandhogs. Recently sober, Jimmy wanted to bring the AA message to his fellow workers and asked the union's business agent and officers to support the development of a formal program.

During his recovery, Jimmy had become acquainted with the growing employee assistance movement within New York. Spurred on by funds from the National Institute on Alcohol Abuse and Alcoholism, New York State developed a network of consultants who promoted program adoption and implementation to both large and small businesses, unions, and professional associations (Trice, Beyer, and Coppess 1981; Johnson 1981). One union that adopted and implemented a program during this period was the longshoremen, another occupation noted for intemperate drinking (Mars 1987; Pilcher 1972), and Jimmy was well acquainted with the longshoreman Jack H., who administered that program. The longshoreman was a prominent member of the state's employee assistance network and eventually became a national leader and advocate for the development of union-sponsored programs. Jimmy included Jack in his early meetings with the union's business agent, Richard Fitzsimmons, who acknowledges that "he gave us a lot of inside information about helping. . . . A lot of credit should go to Jack."

Union officials, particularly those representing intemperate drinking cultures, find it politically difficult to adopt alcoholism programs because they fear that, if they implement the programs, their members will not reelect them (Trice and Beyer 1982). This is particularly true when programs use disciplinary actions in order to overcome the psychodynamics of alcoholics' denial of having a drinking problem. Consequently, union officials elected to protect, rather than threaten, workers' jobs must reframe programs as sources of union support. In their discussions with Fitzsimmons, Jimmy and Jack helped him to reframe the program as fulfilling the union's fraternal obligation to help its members, many of whom remained unemployed because of their alcohol problems. When later discussing his motives for having adopted the program, the business agent said:

We had problems. Lots of guys who were close to me killed themselves by drinking. My initial reaction was that the politics weren't too good. But Jimmy explained how drinking is a sickness and how some of these guys could have been helped. I realized that just like you use the Welfare Fund to put guys in the hospitals for other problems you could do the same for drinking problems. That is an officer's job. No matter what the problem is, the guy is a dues paying member. If he has a problem on the job—a problem with overtime or the boss coming down on him for taking too long with coffee—it is the same kind of problem. . . . Helping the guy is part of representation. Whether it's helping him get into a hospital or his overtime, that is what we are paid to do.

In order to show his support for the adopted alcoholism program, Fitzsimmons provided Jimmy and the other AA sandhogs some office space and put out a policy stating that alcoholism is a disease and declaring the union's commitment to helping its members and their families recover from their alcohol problems. He also negotiated with the contractors to provide some funding for the program and, in return, he promised that, if the contractors would refer workers for treatment instead of disciplining them, the sandhogs would stop drinking in the tunnels.

Although the formal leadership of the sandhogs' alcoholism program has changed hands several times since the seventies, its structure and beliefs about helping coworkers have remained stable.[7] Despite its economic ups and downs, the program looks much the same as when Jimmy and his fellow AA members set it up. Although the program is based on AA's beliefs, the sandhogs have created a structure that reflects their own occupational beliefs as well: it underscores the sandhogs' communal obligations to protect one another. The program follows naturally from the AA's calling to perform twelfth-step work; that is, it consists of a network of recovering sandhogs who remain sober by helping other sandhogs achieve sobriety. Formally, the program has a director who is a member of the AA network. A sandhog has always been the program's director, and it is doubtful that the members would accept anyone but another union member in that position. The current director explains:

[7] The program structure has changed over time. Since the seventies, three sandhogs, including Jimmy, have acted as program directors, and they have always been supported by an informal network of AA members. During the mid-eighties, when there were a good number of sandhogs working, the program consisted of the director, two full-time counselors, and the AA network. As employment declined, the program consisted of the director and network members. Eventually, because of the lack of funding, the director's position also became unpaid. To prevent confusion in the text, I refer to the program as consisting of program and network because the counselors were also network members.

If we brought in what they call a "professional" person . . . an outside social worker to run the program, you might as well not have a program. . . . [The members] wouldn't consider it their program unless a sandhog was running it. Remember, I talked about the sandhogs being very close with a lot of camaraderie. In a lot of areas, they only trust sandhogs. For them, . . . the best model is a guy from the union that they trust and know has had a recovery through the program. . . . You're not going to have that sense of trust and camaraderie unless you're part of it. . . . You can't go out . . . and make believe, "Gee, I want to be one of you guys." They're not going to believe him.

AA members, because they are actively involved in maintaining their own sobriety, have a greater sense of calling for, a deeper involvement with, and a stronger commitment to, alcoholism work than non-AAs (Blum, Roman and Tootle 1988). The men who comprise the sandhog AA network are likewise highly committed to their roles in helping their fellow union members. The director and network members see in alcoholism work a sense of mission, claiming to do it in order to "give something back to the union" that has helped them. But they also do it for themselves. As one network member candidly put it, "I do this for myself. Helping other drunks is the only way I can keep my sobriety. If I don't do it, I'll die."

In addition, because the program is chronically short of money, the director and network members willingly pick up the slack by paying for many of its expenses. These include phone calls to treatment facilities, gas for transporting members to and from AA meetings, and packs of cigarettes as well as the many other items needed by those in rehabilitation. As the current director commented about his own role, "You have to do it for the right reasons. . . . You can't do it for the money. . . . You are entitled to a union member's pay and no more. . . . Many of the unions got into it because [a member] was an ex-drunk, knew the particular union, knew the members and was really concerned about helping them. Those are the right reasons."

Unlike management programs, which use discipline to overcome the alcoholic's denial of his or her illness, the sandhogs proclaim that their program does not include "job jeopardy" because they are obligated to protect one another. Sandhogs who foolishly risk gang members' lives are unlikely to be recruited to the gangs. Similarly, late-stage alcoholics who may not be trusted to act safely are unlikely to be recruited by the gangs. The sandhog AAs reach out to these men vowing to help them. One sandhog AA is explicit about this: "We stick with a guy no matter what. We don't threaten his job. We keep working with him until he gets it. After all, he's a member of the union and we're here to help him. That's what unions are for and that makes us different from these management programs." By vowing to stick with alcoholic co-workers, the AAs recommit themselves by their own exemplary behavior to the occupational community's basic assumptions.

Rather than threatening co-workers, the AAs seek to attract them to their way of life by acting as examples, living a sober life so that others who suffer from drinking problems will know that it is possible to live without alcohol.

I am an example because I maintain my sobriety. . . . I can show that I can function in society without drinking or being drunk, without saying anything. People [who] knew me when I was a drunkard know I'm not drinking. . . . [Someone who acts as an example is] a guy that's going to work every day, doing the right things with his family, is pretty honest about how he feels, . . . [someone] I would like to emulate, speaking his piece at a union meeting regardless of who it offends and trying to be as honest and as responsible as he can in any situation.

When AA members drink, they call it "slipping." Slipping, although a fairly frequent occurrence in AA (Gellman 1964; Ogborne and Bornet 1982), is a serious violation of the group's norms. Typically, AAs respond to slippers by helping them to reconstruct the events encouraging them to drink, and this interaction serves to remind the other AAs of "what it was like" and the need to be ever-vigilant about their own sobriety (Rudy 1986). When a previous program director began drinking again, the AAs made him give up his directorship and go back to the tunnel. They reasoned that, having slipped, he could no longer act as an example for others: "You didn't get drunk the day you picked up a drink; you got drunk two months before or two years before. . . . If you have seriously been working in the [AA] program, you wouldn't pick up the drink. . . . If I pick up a drink, how can I tell you how great sobriety is? . . . What good am I to you?" By demanding that the director give up his directorship, the AAs underlined the seriousness of his deviant behavior and re-emphasized that being an example is synonymous with sobriety.

In addition to attracting members by example, the network teaches its recruits how to become sober, getting them into treatment or AA and "working the program." Often it means recounting one's own story as an example. As one AA aptly put it, "As a facilitator I am just teaching them what I learned from what I went through. What I know works." It is also likened to an endless tape recording, repeating over and over, "Alcoholics can't drink. If you follow the AA program, you can live a sober life. This is what happened to me." AAs act as facilitators on the job when they tell their stories, hold mini-AA meetings, and in numerous ways support one another through the day. When they direct union members to rehabilitation or take new recruits to meetings, they also act as facilitators. As one network member commented, "Now there was a new voice on the block saying, 'You don't have to be a drunk to do this job.' "

In the unfreezing stage, New York City's economic disruptions created widespread unemployment within the sandhogs, providing them with an opportunity to rethink their beliefs about drinking and work. Jimmy M., a sandhog who was also a member of AA, successfully reframed the community's unemployment problems by arguing that many of those who remained unemployed suffered from alcohol problems and that it was the union's obligation to help them to become sober. He convinced the sandhogs' business agent to support the alcoholism program, which combines AA's beliefs about alcoholism and the sandhogs' mutual aid commitment to protecting one another. The program is built around a network of AAs who seek to attract other alcoholics to the network by acting as sober examples and, thus, eventually transform their drinking culture into a sober one.

Toward Temperance

Most cultural change processes fail because, once a program of action is adopted, organizations fail to implement the necessary actions (Trice and Beyer 1993). This is generally a failure to mobilize the resources necessary for keeping the new beliefs alive. The most important resources needed for the change effort are leaders to teach the new beliefs, recruits to learn the new beliefs, and time to ensure that the new beliefs are reinforced so that they eventually become taken for granted in adherents' daily lives.

Intemperate drinking cultures are not transformed over night. Indeed, the transformation experienced by the sandhogs was a tedious process of recruiting individual members to the AA network and teaching them the ways of sobriety. Within the sandhogs, this stage lasted from the program's adoption in the late seventies until the late eighties, when the members looked around and realized that the composition of the gangs had been transformed so that those working were either sober AAs or social drinkers, who did not drink in the tunnels and consumed alcohol in moderation during nonworking hours.

The transformation of the sandhogs' intemperate drinking culture proceeded on two levels, the individual and the organizational. The change process on these two levels did not proceed sequentially but was more complex. Individual sandhogs were recruited to the AA network, where they eventually learned to live sober lives by helping other sandhogs to become and remain sober. Their individual sobriety directly affected the organizational level in two critical ways. First, as sober workers, their presence on the gangs affected the group's dynamics so that the remainder of the gang were less apt to drink in the tunnels and were encouraged to go home after work rather than to the bars. The program director explained it this way:

> You have a gang of ten or twelve guys and maybe two of those guys sober up. Once you make a change within that little group, then the rest of the group changes. They don't all become sober because they are not all drunks. Some maybe drank only because these two drunks did and they wanted to be part of the crowd. All of a sudden these two guys changed. Now they are dressing and going home and they may be driving three or four other guys. . . . If those guys aren't ready, they're up the creek. I think that is basically what happened.

Second, as sober sandhogs, many of them chose to become more involved in the union and actively assumed leadership roles by becoming gang leaders, stewards, and walking bosses. In these capacities, they made sure that either AAs, social drinkers, or intemperate drinkers who were making an effort to become sober were hired on the gangs. In this way, they reinforced changes at the individual level. For instance, one AA recounted how the AA bosses gave him a chance when he was recently sober: "When I got sober, I had to learn my trade. The guys who were sober would put me onto a job. Up at Van Cortland, [the foreman] asked me, 'Can you run a jack leg?' I said, 'No, but I am willing to learn.' Before I got sober, I would have said, 'No fucking way.' . . . He showed me and took his time. It was a gift from God." In this manner, the AA network, because it increasingly controlled the jobs, was eventually able to transform their intemperate culture by sobering up one person at a time. Thus, as more and more members learned the value of temperance, the old drinking rituals became meaningless and as fewer and fewer sandhogs participated in them, gradually lost their symbolic hold over the community.

Occupational socialization can take a variety of forms (Van Maanen and Schein 1979); because the AA program is essentially based upon individual conversion (Rudy 1986) and the union depends upon the gangs to train its members, the sandhogs' alcoholism program uses the gangs to individually teach newcomers to AA about sobriety. In recruiting and socializing recruits to the new temperance beliefs, the AA network recognizes that being a sandhog is a salient identity for occupational members and plays upon their fears of losing that identity in order to transform them into sober sandhogs. In this transformation process, the AAs bring all of the ritual elements into play, except that drinking alcohol now symbolizes the destruction of the individual and his communal bonds with community members. In their interactions with the new recruits, the AAs highlight the degree to which the sandhog's drinking is no longer fun, has made him a poor craftsman, and made him an untrustworthy gang member. They also emphasize that continued drinking will ultimately lead to death or loss of employment. At the same time, the AAs express their willingness to stick by him no matter how miserable his life becomes and, thus, underscoring the sandhogs' basic assumptions that the world is dangerous and that sandhogs, particularly those who are sober, protect one another through thick and thin. In addition, they tell him that by joining the AA network, recovery and a joyous life are possible without alcohol. Within the context of the gang, then, the AAs provide recruits with a new salient identity, which has some continuity with their old occupational image. Now, however, the recruits believe that "one does not have to drink in order to be a sandhog" and know that they can manage the danger, still have fun, and be excellent craftsmen without drinking. This individual rite of passage occurs in three stages.

Recruiting New Members
The recruitment stage consists of recruiting the suspected alcoholic sandhog into the network, and it is characterized by network members identifying and confronting suspected alcoholics. During this stage, the AAs confront the recruit's sense of identity, telling him that drinking is killing him and that drinking is threatening his opportunities to work. The goal is to convince the suspected alcoholic to give the AA philosophy a chance.

Within the sandhogs, gossip, socially virtuous talk which asserts group norms (Gluckman 1963), plays an important role in identifying the suspected alcoholic. Sandhogging is characterized by an intense gossip network, and the AAs co-opted it to their own ends. Within this small union, everyone knows everyone else's business, and the AA network was constantly buzzing with stories about who was and was not working, who was having problems with his wife and children, who was not performing on the gangs, and how and where individuals were drinking. The gossip was evident in the hog houses and in network members' frequent phone conversations with the director. Inevitably, the AAs believed that they knew quite well who was in trouble because of drinking.

Within the context of the sandhog AA network, trouble took on specific meanings (e.g., Emerson and Messinger 1977). It meant trouble with the job, which was indicated by not showing up for work, inability to get onto a gang, doing something dangerous in the hole, drinking on the job, and sleeping it off in the hog house or tunnel. It also meant trouble outside work: wives' frequent complaints to the AAs about their husbands, arrests for driving while intoxicated, inability to pay bills, and fighting. And it also meant physical trouble, indicated by a host of alcoholism-related symptoms, including chronic gastrointestinal pain, vomiting, bleeding and blackouts. Knowledge of such troubles associated with awareness of heavy and prolonged drinking was an indication to the network that someone had an alcohol problem; their suspicion, however, was confirmed when they confronted the suspect and he blamed all of his troubles on something or someone other than himself. This is called "having an attitude." "It is never his fault. It is always the old lady's, the cop's, the boss's, someone else's. It is never that he does anything to create the situation. It is never that he is mean, angry, or drunk." Based upon their assessment of trouble, the AAs would approach the individual and attempt to recruit him into the network. One network member described this recruitment process:

> You just know when to approach a guy. For example, when he has not shown up for four or five days and is feeling like hell. [The network member approaches the person in the hog house at their lockers before their shift.] I tell them, "It does not have to be like this. If you want to go away, I can make a couple of phone calls [to the counselors and treatment agencies] and you can go without anyone knowing." Often these guys are ready to go because they have had enough. Sometimes they have passed out in the tunnel, and they are scared. Sometimes they have been arrested for driving while intoxicated or they have been in a fight. Sometimes they just come and ask for help. Sometimes they ask saying it's for their son or daughter. Usually the trouble is on the job.

The sharing of rides to work is a common phenomenon within the union, and the AAs would offer a suspected alcoholic a ride to show that they could be relied upon in a pinch. Such rides were also an opportunity for the AAs to act as examples and offer the suspected alcoholic help. On one occasion, I witnessed a network member negotiating with a young sandhog who was hitch-hiking a ride to Pennsylvania Station because he had been convicted of DWI. The network member knew about his DWI conviction because one of the miners had told him about it. On our way out of the yard, he offered the young sandhog a lift and casually asked, "Why are you walking?" My field notes describe the conversation in the car.

> C. [the young sandhog] responds: "I got busted for DWI." He says the cops could have gotten him for resisting arrest but stuck

him with DWI. He was sleeping in a parked car when the cops asked what he was doing. He was also racing the motor. His tale is confused, but the upshot is that he had bad-mouthed the police who arrested him. C. has been to the DWI classes and claims that he does not drink much. AA asks him if he is going to any meetings. C. denies he has a drinking problem and says that it was all the cop's fault. AA talks to C. about one of C.'s cousins who is in the program and points out he could go to meetings with him. C. says he does not drink that much. AA assures him that they will get him. After leaving him at the station, AA told me that C.'s father was also an alcoholic sandhog who died in tragic circumstances from alcohol abuse and reassured me, "We will get him, though. You wait and see. He is starting to hurt now. The drinking is starting to cause him problems. When he is hurting enough, he will come around."

According to studies of AA affiliation, alcoholics will not join until they have experienced intense feedback about their drinking behavior and come to see themselves as licked (Gellman 1964; Maxwell 1984; Robinson 1979; Rudy 1986; Trice, 1957; Trice and Roman 1970b). Likewise, network members and counselors believe that alcoholics will give AA a try when they are "hurting enough" and they will sober up after they "hit their bottom." Hurting and hitting bottom are not necessarily the same. Many sandhogs tried AA when they were experiencing a great deal of physical and emotional pain because of their drinking, but, when they started feeling better, returned to drinking. Hitting bottom, on the other hand, occurs when they take their last drink, something that can be known only retrospectively, after they have learned to stay in the network. A twenty-year-old, who had been drinking since he was eleven and had been sober for twenty-two days, explained that drinking was no longer fun and that the hurting drove him into the program:

My father called [the director]. . . . I just got tired of hurting. Like the saying goes, "I got sick and tired of being sick and tired." I got sick and tired of waking up and not knowing what had happened to me. Look at my hand. [Shows his badly scarred and swollen hand.] I did that in a blackout. I don't know what happened. When I was drinking, I'd get up the next morning and start all over so I could forget. I just got sick and tired. I like how I feel now. I don't like having a cold but I like how I feel. When I was drinking, I wouldn't know I had a cold. Since I've been sober, I feel all these things I never felt before. I even took a girl out the other night. I mean I didn't piss on anybody in front of me or anything. I knew what I was doing. I was scared but acted like a perfect gentleman. I took her home and gave her a peck on the cheek and ran like hell. Me! Shit, I never took a girl out before. No, I like how I feel.

Frequently, the hurting that most often drove the sandhogs to the program was job-related. Over and over they told me that when they first tried the program, they were already in trouble with their families and in physical pain and were finally prompted to go because they were afraid of being unable to get on a gang and losing their union book. Their decision to do so was reinforced by the examples set by the AAs. A sandhog who attributed the beginning of his sobriety to a seizure in the tunnel explained: "When I was drinking, I took a look at [an AA] and some of the other guys and they were laughing. . . . I couldn't understand it. Someone not drinking and being happy. I was miserable when I wasn't drinking. I was scared. . . . I really wanted to be like them. I wanted what they had. That was the power of example, them being happy . . . not letting things bother them that much."

Suspected alcoholic sandhogs were driven to give the AA network a chance when they were hurting enough: when they found that drinking was no longer fun, and they began to fear that their drinking was jeopardizing their place in the gangs. In their interactions with the AA network, the suspected alcoholics learned that there was hope. From the examples set by the AAs, they learned that it is possible to have fun without drinking and that being a good craftsman does not require drinking. They also learned from these interactions that the AA network is willing to stick by them even when their gangs have abandoned them.

Socializing New Recruits
In the socialization stage, the recruits to AA are betwixt and between (Van Gennep [1908] 1960; Turner 1969); they are aware that they must change but uncertain about what it means to be a recov-

ering alcoholic and live a sober life. Consequently, the socialization stage was a dangerous passage fraught with slips; in order to negotiate it safely, the newcomers had to learn to live by AA's twelve steps and to trust the AA network. In their interactions with the AAs, they learned what it meant to be an alcoholic and constructed their new identity as sober sandhogs.

According to AA wisdom, anyone who diligently sticks to the twelve steps can gain sobriety. The sandhogs, however, experienced intense pressures to return to drinking, making the passage from drinking to sobriety particularly difficult. On and off the job, they were continuously confronted with the easy camaraderie of their old drinking groups. Indeed, because the AAs sought to attract co-workers to sobriety rather than telling them not to drink, there was relatively little friction between them and the intemperate drinkers who knew them as reliable gang members before they sobered up. For instance, one miner, sober three to four years, jokingly related that when he was coming out of the hole one evening, the others were passing around beers and he took one not realizing what had happened. At home, they also experienced intense pressures to drink because many of their family members drank. For example, one young sandhog asked the director to get him into a rehabilitation program because he could not bear to be at home and watch his older brother, sister, and friends sitting around drinking. He commented, "In the entrance to my building, there are usually six guys selling dope. My brother says you can't live in this neighborhood without using drugs."

Some sandhogs learned to live within the safety of the AA network more quickly than others did. For example, one sandhog told me how he broke his foot shortly after first going to AA. "At first I felt self-pity but then I realized it must have been for some good reason. The whole time my foot was in a cast I went to three or four AA meetings a day. I'd go to one in the Bronx in the morning, Manhattan in the afternoon, back up to Queens in the evening or whatever. As a result I got better faster. So, see, it really was all for the good. God works in mysterious ways." For many, however, learning to live within the network was a long, drawn-out ordeal. One network member joked about getting drunk every year for eight years on his AA anniversary. His experience highlights that the AA network, true to its word, never gives up on those in trouble.

I bounced in and out like a yoyo. I just couldn't get it in my head that I could function without the drink. . . . They had the program going; . . . I was going to [AA] meetings with [the counselor] and a lot of other people. . . . I always knew they were there, the sober people on the jobs. . . . Eventually it finally hit me that I didn't have to drink to do this job. . . . If my union, the sandhogs, hadn't put together this program and gotten a lot of guys sober, I wouldn't have been able to make it.

Another said, "Every time I stopped hanging out with the guys in AA on the job, I got drunk."

Network members employed a variety of tactics to keep individuals within the network's sober embrace. In each of the hog houses, the AAs had their lockers together and kept the recruit within their embrace by moving his locker into their area and making sure he had an AA buddy either on his gang or in his work area. On the job, the AAs expressed their support for one another in a variety of symbolic gestures—a wink, a nod, and a smile to one another as the cage dropped into the hole or a cheerful toot of the crane's whistle. "It says we are here and we will make it through the day. AA is the language of the heart."

AA network solidarity was also expressed in clowning and joking, which highlights that sobriety can be playful. One afternoon, for example, some AAs were setting up a meeting date with a newcomer and joked that maybe they should not have gotten him into the network because he had "changed so much for the better." The newcomer then recounted how his girlfriend poured him a drink and he told her, "I don't drink anymore. I take it one day at a time. She sure was surprised."

Every day there were also scores of mini-AA meetings on the job, a potent symbol to newcomers that the network is always ready to help them negotiate the dangerous passage to sobriety. One AA network member likened alcoholism to "an immunological deficiency with a defunct enzyme sending a message to one's brain. The message says, 'I am OK! I am not an alcoholic. I can drink.' The AA meetings on and off the job are necessary to interrupt this message and say, 'You are an alcoholic!' " Another told me how he was ready to crown his foreman with a two-by-four when another AA showed up. They discussed the first AA's anger and the other AA advised him to "let it go." The first AA believed that "if he had not shown up I would have lost my sobriety for sure. God works in mysterious ways."

Within the tunnels, the mini-AA meetings taught newcomers that they did not have to drink in order to manage their fear. For instance, one AA explained that, when he was first learning to stay sober, he was scared to death in the tunnels. "The foreman was AA, and his power of example was reassuring. My helper on the drill, an AA, advised me, 'Calm down! Relax! Take it easy. You'll make it.' He [said he had] felt the same way I did [when he was a newcomer] and somebody else helped him. . . . [Another guy on a different gang] came over and told us he was AA. He would come over and talk to us two or three times a day."

Within the occupational community, the AAs taught the recruits how to live AA's twelve-step program by continually reinterpreting their behavior within its philosophy. The first lesson the AAs taught newcomers, for instance, is not to drink, no matter what happens. One afternoon, I accompanied a network member and a young worker who was afraid of relapsing as they searched for a rehabilitation program. The hunt took us from Manhattan to Queens, out to Long Island and back. The AA could not find a program that would take the young man. Throughout the trip, the AA continually reassured the young man that he could make it. "You don't have to drink. Your dad [he is AA] doesn't drink anymore and look at the problems he's got. Your old man has guts. He sticks it out because the program helps him. You got twenty-two days in already. You've gotten through today so far. Drinking is only gonna make things worse—not better. If you feel like drinking, go to a meeting."

The AAs also instructed the recruit in how to work the twelve steps. For instance, one network member, upon returning from a sandhog's apartment, related how he reviewed with him the fourth step, which requires that members make a searching and fearless moral inventory of themselves.

He was wrecking his apartment because he had four months of sobriety and couldn't understand why his wife wouldn't come back. I told him he was lucky he was able to see his kids let alone have his wife back. The wife [had] found him in bed with his girlfriend and threatened divorce. Now that he is sober, he has the "poor-me's." He had a stiff cock and no one to take care of it. I told him to relieve himself with his hand. Poor me! I told him to clean up the place and then worked on the fourth step with him. Next time I'll work on the fifth step with him. Sometimes you have to be hard on these guys or they won't listen.

Frequently, AAs tell dramatic stories about hitting bottom before they really started getting sober (Trice and Roman 1970a). The stories are fraught with broken families, lost opportunities, spent fortunes, pain, anguish, and despair. Looking back, the AAs pinpoint a catastrophe that finally turned them around: a seizure, an accident, a divorce, or inability to work. One sandhog described his turning point:

I'd just come out of [treatment]. . . . I had the horrors. Everybody drank on this gang. . . . We were on a scaffold, 240 feet off the ground. . . . We were pumping grout. . . . We hit like 2500 pounds of pressure. We got sprayed. I had it in my eyes. . . . We let ourselves down. This guy [M.] was worst up there. . . . We put him on the cage. . . . [After work] I had to stay with these guys because I had no other way of getting home. . . . By two o'clock they polished off two cases of beer and I was drinking soda. . . . They said where is M.? We come back the next day and hear he is dead. . . . He must have fell out of the cage. No one ever knew what the hell happened. But it scared me. I didn't want to drink again.

In the end, however, the recruits claimed that they learned to stay sober because of the AA network. Each time a recruit was tempted to pick up a drink, the network members were there to reinterpret his behavior within the framework of AA. As one of them explained, "If it weren't for the guys on the job, I'd be drinking yet. They help you just talking to you."

Incorporation into Their Helping Role
In the incorporation stage, the recruits become fully committed to their helping role. They act as examples, thinking of themselves as recovering alcoholics and helping others who are in trouble with alcohol. As one recruit to the network remarked, "Six months later,

another guy who was in bad shape started asking me about the program, and I started talking to him. It was my turn to help someone else, and now he's helping someone else. That's the way it works."

Incorporation into the helping role, however, did not occur all at once; rather, it occurred slowly as recruits achieved one day of sobriety at a time. Upon reflection, they realized that they had gained sobriety and were part of the network. They now identified themselves as alcoholics, typically contrasting themselves with those who were still drinking intemperately. As one stated it, "I know what I am. I am an alcoholic. The difference is I know what I am. They don't; they are sick." As sober sandhogs and members of the AA network, they believed that it was their obligation to support one another as well as help newcomers gain sobriety. They claimed to do it for themselves, believing it is the only way to stay sober, and to give something back to their union and those who have helped them.

Again, it was in their helping role that the AAs had their greatest impact upon transforming the sandhogs' intemperate drinking culture at the organizational level. As they became sober and began helping others, many also chose to assume more active leadership roles in the union. Like Jimmy M. before them, those AAs who became gang leaders hired sober workers—AAs, social drinkers, and those intemperate drinkers trying to become sober. They eventually came to control the gangs and emphasized that one no longer had to drink intemperately to be a sandhog.

Refreezing the Culture:
Reinforcing the New Temperance Beliefs

In the final stage of transforming the intemperate drinking culture, the new temperance beliefs are reinforced and amplified within the occupational community so that they eventually become taken for granted. The sandhogs' intemperate drinking culture has been transformed; community members no longer drink in the tunnels. One sandhog observed, "We went from a culture of drinking to a culture of sobriety. Now, if you are drunk on the job you stand out. At one time, if you were sober you stood out. . . . I don't see any gangs any more that come out of the tunnel and all go out to the bar and drink and stay out all night."

Another estimates, "On the Staten Island job, every one on the job was either AA or a social drinker. . . . Eighty percent of foremen, walking bosses, and shop stewards were in the program." Similarly, the sandhogs currently working on the Water Tunnel Number 3— approximately sixty men—are either AAs or social drinkers. The program director, who works as the hog house man, remarked, "Things have really changed. Nobody is drinking in the tunnels anymore. They don't even drink in the hog house much anymore. Most of the time, they come up, change their clothes, and are out of there in ten, fifteen minutes."

The sandhogs stabilized the new temperance beliefs by reinforcing the belief that one does not have to drink in order to be a sandhog and underscoring that helping other union members, regardless of their problems, was the real essence of being a sandhog and the bedrock of communal solidarity. Reinforcement and amplification of these beliefs occurred in several ways.

First, the new beliefs were reinforced by the union officers who encouraged the gang leaders to hire the newly sober. The sandhogs' business manager, who had supported the program at some risk to his position, said,

> You get so Goddamn proud of a guy when you see him completely turn himself around. . . . Five years ago, the foreman would not have hired him. . . . Now he is searching this guy out because he is off the booze. . . . You see guys nobody would have touched with a ten-foot pole, and now they are able to get a job any place. . . . [Today, a foreman who is a social drinker and has] a guy who is screwed up will mention three or four names to him of sober people. These people are held up to him as examples.

Such actions are visible demonstrations that one does not have to drink in order to be a sandhog, especially in a tight labor market where sandhog jobs are difficult to obtain.

Second, the stories gang members tell one another have changed. They used to be supportive of the old intemperate drinking rituals, but now they highlight the necessity of sobriety. Gang members still tell the old stories, but now those stories are told with an emphasis on how foolhardy alcohol used to make them act, highlighting the contrast between their new sense of community and the old. I was told the following story by an AA network member. In the old days, the story would have emphasized the sandhogs' hard-working macho self-image; now it is used to show how being drunk on the job created an unsafe work environment:

> For a while, we had a barge on the river and a conveyer belt dumping the muck into it. One night in the middle of the winter, the hogs working on the barge got drunk and loaded it un-evenly. The next morning one end of the barge was slipping under the water and the other was sticking up in the air. The hogs, hung over and some still drunk, ran out in T-shirts with their "muck sticks" and tried to even out the load before it sunk. Only a bunch of drunks would think that they could do that as the barge sank deeper into the water.

Now gang members also tell new stories about what it means to be sober. One network member, who made a career out of showing his peers that you do not have to drink in order to have fun, ex-plained:

> They used to have the drunk stories. Now they are telling all these sober stories about me. . . . Like those clippings from the *Daily News* showing all the crazy stunts and this recent TV broadcast of my brother and me walking barefoot on hot coals. . . . That is something new they talk about, and they say, "This fucking guy is just as fucking crazy as ever." It's an image I don't mind projecting; it's a fun image. Nobody's being hurt and a lot of people are being helped because of it.

Third, in recognizing that sobriety gives them options, the sober sandhogs, by choosing to stay within the community and to take on new occupational responsibilities, reconfirmed that one need not drink in order to be a sandhog. As one sandhog expressed it, "As a drunk, I never saw any options! But sobriety has given me options." In their recovery, they discover that they have grown beyond the boundaries of their old community and they no longer live in a mar-ginal world. By renouncing alcohol, adopting a repentant role, and demonstrating their sobriety, they become respectable within the larger community. Consequently, when they become sober, some members say that sandhogging "isn't your identity anymore; it's just your job." A well-paying job that allows them to do many things—go to school and meetings, have families and friends, move out of the old neighborhoods, buy a home, and be a "good union member." Exercising such options reinforces their identity as sober AAs.

Although the AAs recognized that sobriety has provided them other employment options, many chose to remain sandhogs. In choosing to stay, they reconfirmed that pride of craft does not need to be expressed in drinking rituals. Rather, they expressed it through hard work and by becoming more involved in running the union. As one member expressed it,

> Drunk sandhogs are hard workers and, when you sober them up, you get even more work out of them. A lot of them are great bosses. Many of our foremen are in the program. . . . Guys that hadn't worked steady in three years; now they are foremen. . . . A guy who was dead drunk is a shop steward. . . . This was all through sobriety. They didn't [just] stop drinking; they changed their personalities; they weren't fighting anymore. . . . Now they are assets to the union.

Fourth, the AA network stabilized the new temperance beliefs by underscoring that the alcoholism program is really a reflection of the sandhogs' basic assumptions about protecting one another, especially in moments of need. They did so by expanding the program from a focus on alcoholism to assisting members with any personal problem. According to the director,

> When I say drunks taking care of drunks it sounds like I'm only talking about alcohol. But, we've put people into treatment for anemia, anorexia, mental problems. We've had people in Gamblers Anonymous. . . . We have made all kinds of referrals for marital counseling. We've had teenagers, court appearances for DWI, and so many other areas. . . . We wouldn't have gotten into these areas without first getting the trust of the people with the alcoholism program. The guy got sober and started to look at his family. He never knew his kid was screwed up. He would never

have asked for help for the kid, but he knew us and trusted us. He calls and says, "My son is having trouble in school; I think he's on grass. Is there a place to send him?" . . . "My wife and I aren't getting along. Is there a place where we can go?" . . . [Or, another sandhog will ask a sober guy on the gang], "You got sober through the program. . . . I'm all screwed up. Household Finance is after me; I'm in hock up to my ears. What do I do?" He says, "Go talk to [Bill] over at the program. He's got lots of referral lists. He can give you a hand." That's how it works, one union member helping another.

One network member commented, "Today, no one says bad things about the program because it has touched every member's family."

Finally, the sandhogs have stabilized their new temperance beliefs by underscoring that helping others is the basis for building solidarity within the labor movement. Just as Jack H. helped Jimmy to develop their alcoholism program, the AAs have acted as examples for other unions with intemperate drinking cultures. Initially, they helped other unions by twelve-stepping their members. As the director of the sandhogs' alcoholism program noted, "There's a lot of construction unions in the city that don't have [alcohol] programs. . . . The sandhogs hang out with a lot of construction workers. If someone calls us, we take care of them the same as we do with a member of our own union."

These interactions often lead the AAs to help other unions develop their own programs. One afternoon I attended a meeting with the sandhog program director and a member from one of the city's maintenance unions interested in starting a program. After the meeting, the director told me that the maintenance union member was starting a program for the right reason:

To help his fellow union members. That's the right concept. Somebody was telling me about a guy in California, who runs a construction program and is running all over the state training union members to run programs for themselves. [Somebody] said to me, "Is he crazy? Why don't he get them into his own program? . . . [Somebody] doesn't understand that he is supposed to help other unions get straight and that he isn't supposed to build an empire. . . . It's the same thing that would have happened to AA. If AA went out for money, it wouldn't work. It's the same with these programs. You do it to keep your sobriety and see people help themselves.

Despite their accomplishments, the sandhogs are aware that their temperate drinking culture remains fragile and requires continual reinforcement. One sandhog remarked, "Some of them still tell the old stories about drinking and fighting and the kids want to live up to that old image. But that is changing. It takes time." The AAs ask themselves, "What will happen when money becomes available for completion of the water tunnel and the union puts a lot of inexperienced workers in the hole? Will they revert to the old ways, drinking in order to cope with the horrors of the tunnel?" Optimistically, the AAs point to current conditions and assert, "We'll never go back to the old way of doing things." According to one network member, "It used to be that if you were drunk in the tunnels, the bosses would cover you up, send you home. Now, they say, 'If you're going to act like that, don't bother coming down.' " The AAs point out that the work has changed, and it is easier to enforce such expectations. Whereas twenty years ago there were large gangs with three hundred or more men on a project, today gangs are small with only fifty men on a project. Another network member stated: "It's a difference in the generations. It's the guys in the program are running gangs— the walking bosses, the foremen. . . . Like years ago it was barroom gangs, drunks. . . . Three years from now, when it breaks big, you'll see guys hiring AA guys. And they better know what the fuck they are doing too. . . . In the past, you went for nationalities, for alcoholics, and now you're going for sober people." Still, the sandhogs recognize that they must be vigilant lest they slip back into their old habits.

Conclusion

The sandhogs transformed their intemperate drinking culture into a temperate one by changing the meaning its members attached to drinking. They redefined their intemperate drinking as alcoholism and claimed that it was undermining the community's survival. As proof of this claim, they pointed to the unemployed sandhogs, who, unable to find work, spent their time in the bars. Within this context, the community imported AA's belief system into the union as a mechanism for helping alcoholic members become sober. Although the program's temperance message was initially resisted by members, the sandhogs' business agent justified it by arguing that it reflected the union's basic responsibility to help its members, a moral obligation that transcended an individual's right to drink.

Initially, the alcoholism program focused upon transforming the identities of individual sandhogs from drinkers to sober sandhogs. In transforming their identities, the AA network used the ritual elements in order to build a new set of communal bonds based upon the labor movement's helping ethic. Within the context of the gang, the AAs recruited suspected alcoholics and taught them how to use the principles of AA to become sober and cope with the dangers of the tunnels. They repeatedly emphasized to the recruits that drinking was dangerous and that individual survival depended upon helping one another retain their sobriety. This approach transformed the old communal self into a new occupational hero, the sober sandhog: "someone who is a good worker, father, and husband, is a good union member going to meetings and speaking up, is respected for being a decent person, and doing the right things financially."

As the number of sober sandhogs increased, the old intemperate drinking rituals became increasingly meaningless to the community, failing to mark its boundary or to create strong communal bonds among members. Intemperate drinking failed to mark the sandhog communal boundary because the walking bosses and foremen, often newly sober themselves, no longer hired those with whom they drank. Rather, they hired AAs and social drinkers on the basis of a new consciousness of kind marked by temperance.

As intemperate drinking has lost its symbolic hold on the sandhogs, the intentionally enacted rituals of helping have become more salient for the strengthening of their communal bonds. As AA members enact these rituals with one another on and off the job, they have come to define themselves within their helping role. They define being a good union member as someone who is not drinking, is going to AA meetings, and helping other sandhogs remain sober. Likewise, they look to the other AAs to help keep them sober on and off the job. Within the union, this role has also been extended to helping sandhogs and their families cope with a wide range of personal problems. These helping relationships reenergize those who participate in them, reconfirming the community's basic assumptions and renewing their communal bonds. Similarly, the extension of the helping role to other unions highlights for the sandhogs their obligations to, and solidarity with, the labor movement.

By transforming their intemperate drinking culture, then, the sandhogs have realigned their beliefs with those factions of American society that have traditionally defined the drunkard as a folk devil. In doing so, they argue that intemperate drinking, rather than building solidarity, destroys it. And, like earlier generations of workers, they are constructing a new sense of community by rehabilitating the intemperate drinkers in their midst.

6 *From Occupational Intemperance to Temperance: Reconstructing Occupational Community*

The image on which this book opened—the Woodlawn Express speeding out of control, ripping apart the New York City subway tunnel, and maiming passengers—graphically symbolizes the untoward consequences of intemperate occupational drinking: drunken workers create social disorder, endangering people's lives and undermining the public good. Historically, such horror stories, endlessly recounted, fueled America's cycles of temperance reform, driving intemperate drinking from most workplaces by the early part of the twentieth century. Still, some occupational communities continue to construct their lives around intemperate drinking.

The persistence of intemperate drinking must be understood as occupational conformity and, more importantly, as an intentionally initiated ritual for constructing members' sense of community. Consequently, in order for occupational communities with intemperate drinking rituals to transform their cultures into temperate ones, they must redefine their relationship to alcohol so that drinking loses its ritual effects. In this chapter, I briefly summarize my study of the sandhogs' drinking culture and discuss its implications for understanding the transformation of other intemperate occupational drinking cultures.

The Sandhogs: Reconstructing Community

America has experienced a series of temperance reforms in which reformers sought to impose the Puritan notion of sobriety on workers, a lifestyle emphasizing hard work, discipline, orderliness, frugality, responsibility, and moderation in drinking. Historically, temperance advocates, whether religious leaders, politicians, businesspeople, or workers, have defined intemperate drinking as undermining the social order. During the colonial era, for instance, Congregational ministers such as the Mathers preached that demon rum was preventing people from pursuing their callings, prospering, and acting as stewards to the community. After the American Revolution, such leaders as Benjamin Rush, James Madison, and John Adams sought to impose sobriety upon the young republic in order to save it from citizens' excessive consumption of distilled spirits. These guardians of the youthful United States linked temperance and the common good within their definition of the virtuous citizen.

Likewise, businesspeople and labor leaders have pursued a variety of strategies for creating a sober workforce. Businesspeople sought to create disciplined workers and thus increase productivity and profits by banning alcoholic beverages from their shops and factories; some employers refused to hire workers who drank at all, even in the leisure hours. Many workers and unions promoted sobriety as a means of constructing a strong labor movement. Generally, workers and unions promoted temperance through such fraternal organizations as the Washingtonians and Red, Blue, and White Ribbon Clubs, which were designed to transform drunken workers into respectable citizens. For a brief period, temperance was defined as national prohibition and enshrined in federal law as the Eighteenth Amendment. Today, a broad range of institutions, including the National Institute on Alcohol Abuse and Alcoholism, state alcohol authorities, local alcoholism councils, and employee assistance providers continue to support management and labor's efforts to create a sober workforce.

Despite management and labor efforts to promote temperance at work, some occupational communities such as railroaders, assembly-line workers, construction workers, and naval personnel continue to drink intemperately. As the case of the sandhogs illustrates, this persistence occurs because, rather than viewing drinking as destructive of their communal life, members of an intemperate occupational community experience it as a ritual for marking their communal boundary and strengthening their communal bonds. Intemperate drinking among the sandhogs, whether in the tunnels, hog houses, or bars, perfectly expressed the community's basic assumptions to members: occupational survival depends upon members sticking together. Within this framework, intemperate drinking reinforced their consciousness of kind and underscored the obligations they owed one another: sandhogs drank, and they hired those with whom they drank. Thus, they experienced intemperate drinking as an emotionally arousing ritual that strengthened rather than destroyed their communal bonds.

The sandhogs began to transform their intemperate drinking culture in the seventies. The study of their efforts to change their intemperate drinking practices revealed a three-step occupational rite of passage in which the community's relationship to alcohol was redefined as undermining its basic assumptions. In the unfreezing stage, the collapse of their labor market prompted members to reevaluate their obligations to one another and to reconsider the place of intemperate drinking within their community. A well-respected sandhog was able to import AA's beliefs into the community by successfully arguing that unemployed members were suffering from alcoholism and that the union had a basic fraternal obligation to help members regardless of the illness. In the transformation stage, a network of AA sandhogs, through the support of the business manager and eventually through their control of the gangs, recruited and taught individual alcoholics the AA philosophy. As each individual gained sobriety and helped others to attain it and keep it, the old drinking rituals gradually released their grip on the community and the new ethic of temperance took hold of it. In the refreezing stage, the temperance ethic was reinforced and amplified within the community by the union's demonstrated commitment to hiring sober AAs and social drinkers, by the telling of stories that contrasted the new with the old drinking culture and emphasized the foolishness associated with the old drinking rituals, and by broadening the AA network's efforts to help members with other kinds of problems. The sober sandhog gradually replaced the intemperate sandhog as the community's new occupational hero and became a symbol of members' basic obligation to protect one another. As a consequence, the sandhogs now take it for granted that one does not need to drink in order to be a sandhog.

By institutionalizing temperance in their culture, the sandhogs have brought their occupational community into alignment with the national culture of respectability: they have transformed the mythic sandhog into a model of the virtuous citizen, who exercises self-control in the pursuit of his work and acts as a steward for the common good.

Transforming Other Occupational Drinking Cultures

The process revealed by the sandhogs' efforts to transform their intemperate occupational drinking culture has implications for other occupational communities that construct their communal lives around alcohol.

First, theorists debate whether culture simply conforms to the material world or whether beliefs change independently of the material world (e.g., Alexander 1990; Alexander and Seidman 1990). This study suggests that a crisis in the material world may be necessary to create the opportunity for intemperate drinking cultures to be changed, but the crisis itself is not sufficient for cultural transformation to occur. The sandhogs had experienced many similar layoffs in the history of their occupational community, but those economic downturns did not produce changes in their beliefs about intemperate drinking. Before such a change could occur, it was necessary for an occupational leader to reframe the community's economic problems as temperance difficulties and for the union to agree to adopt temperance reform. These findings suggest that other occupational communities will not begin to transform their intemperate drinking cultures until they experience an economic crisis and a community member successfully reframes their material difficulties within temperance beliefs.

Second, the cultural change literature often advocates a top-down approach, only rarely considering the possibilities for transforming work cultures from the bottom up (Wardell 1992). In contrast to the top-down strategy for change of employee assistance programs, this study suggests that a bottom-up strategy may be necessary for changing intemperate occupational drinking cultures, particularly within those communities that exercise a great deal of autonomy over their work and make drinking a symbol of their resistance to management control. Like other occupational communities, the sandhogs, beginning with the Brooklyn Bridge project, staunchly resisted their bosses' efforts to keep alcohol off the job, instead making intemperate drinking rituals a basis of communal solidarity. It was only after the sandhogs themselves began redefining their relationship to alcohol that those drinking rituals eventually lost their symbolic hold over members, failing to mark their communal boundaries and to strengthen their communal bonds.

Third, organizational theorists have highlighted the importance of executive leadership in transforming culture, but they have rarely examined the role of indigenous leaders in cultural transformation (Trice and Beyer 1993). This study suggests that indigenous occupational leaders play a critical role in the transformation of deeply embedded cultural behaviors, such as intemperate drinking. Rank-and-file members rather than the union leadership were the first to become involved with AA, import its philosophy into the sandhogs, and reframe it within the community's basic assumptions. Indeed, the union's business agent's first reaction to the alcoholism program was that the politics of changing members' intemperate drinking practices "were not too good." Nevertheless, he eventually changed his mind about the program once the indigenous leaders made him realize that helping alcoholic members was a union obligation like helping members with medical and job-related problems.

In addition, the study suggests that indigenous occupational leaders must have a sense of mission that compels them to run against the tide of the community's established beliefs and practices. Within the sandhogs, this sense of mission came from members' involvement with AA; psychologically, they felt they had to practice AA's twelve-step program within their occupational community or die. Whether such a sense of mission for transforming intemperate drinking cultures is dependent upon AA membership remains unexamined. For instance, social drinkers may also develop such a sense of mission when it is grounded in an effort to live up to their occupational community's high ideals of brotherhood (Bacharach, Bamberger, and Sonnenstuhl 1994).

Fourth, this study also suggests that, in order for intemperate drinking rituals to be transformed, there must be a great deal of continuity between the old and new occupational cultures. Within the sandhogs, two types of continuity were critical to the transformation process. First, in reframing the community's unemployment problems as alcohol problems, it was necessary to frame the solution to this problem—the alcoholism program—within the context of the sandhogs' basic cultural assumption: survival in a dangerous world depends upon protecting one another. The alcoholism program became another way to fulfill their communal obligations to help one another. Second, in order for the AAs to embed their temperance beliefs in the community, it was also necessary for them to gain control of the gangs, which remain the primary mechanism for teaching sandhogs the appropriate way to behave and for disciplining them for misbehaving. By controlling access to jobs on the gang, the AA network was eventually able to change members' intemperate drinking rituals.

Fifth, while it is intuitively obvious that cultural change occurs only when people enact new beliefs, most change efforts fail to socialize people adequately for the new beliefs to be taken for granted (Trice and Beyer 1993). This is ultimately a failure of resources. The sandhog study suggests that the most important resources for cultural transformation are recruits who are taught the new beliefs and how to enact them in their daily lives. It also suggests that, once individuals are taught the new beliefs, those beliefs must continually be reinforced until they become habits within the occupational community. Within the sandhogs, that reinforcement came from involving the new recruits in helping other sandhogs to attain and keep their sobriety. By transforming one individual at a time, temperance gradually replaced the old drinking rituals.

Although I emphasize the primary importance of recruiting and teaching the new beliefs to individuals, it is also necessary to underscore the importance of time as a critical resource in cultural transformation. In our quick-fix society, executives and administrators often act as though deeply embedded beliefs and behavior will disappear once a program is adopted. As the sandhogs' study suggests, transforming deeply embedded beliefs is not a quick fix. The transformation of the sandhogs' intemperate drinking culture has taken almost two decades; yet the sandhogs worry about whether they will be able to pass it on to future generations. They believe that they can but that it will require them to be continually vigilant, lest the old drinking rituals reemerge with full employment and a new generation of sandhogs.

While this framework for understanding the persistence and transformation of intemperate drinking cultures was generated from one case, the sandhogs, several factors cause me to believe that it is generalizable to other occupational communities that build their lives around intemperate drinking rituals. First, since the publication of an earlier article on the sandhogs (Sonnenstuhl and Trice 1987), workers from other occupational communities who read the article have told me that the sandhogs' experience reflects their own efforts to change their intemperate drinking cultures. Typically, these workers have been AAs doing twelve-step work within their own occupational communities. Second, our recent study of Operation:RedBlock indicates that the railroaders' efforts to change their 150-year-old intemperate drinking culture reflects the sandhogs' experiences (Bacharach, Bamberger, and Sonnenstuhl 1994). In the case of Operation:RedBlock, however, social drinkers and AAs are working together to transform their intemperate drinking culture. Finally, since 1992, I have been working with a new organization, the Labor Assistance Professionals, which is a national coalition of union members involved in the development and administration of alcoholism programs within their locals. Their stories echo the story of the sandhogs' long-term struggle to construct a new sense of community based upon temperance rather than drinking.

Although the transformation process revealed by the sandhogs' study is most easily applied to other unionized occupational communities, it may also have some application to management-sponsored and joint labor-management–sponsored alcoholism and employee assistance programs. Since the late seventies, these programs have relied increasingly upon clinical professionals such as social workers and psychologists rather than upon recovering alcoholics to help employees overcome their problems. As a consequence, some observers have raised questions about the ability of these programs to identify and treat alcoholic employees. One technique for ensuring that these programs are able to identify and treat alcoholics would be to reintegrate AA networks into them. As they did for the sandhogs, these AAs could be relied upon to identify and twelve-step the suspected alcoholics in their midst. In unionized settings, inclusion of such an AA network might also assuage union members' fears that employee assistance is simply another mechanism for identifying and punishing troublemakers. Still, as the recent work of Ames and her colleagues (Ames, Delaney and Janes 1992) suggests, labor-management cooperation on alcohol problems is often difficult to achieve under the best of circumstances, particularly if the union has a deeply embedded intemperate drinking culture.

Despite my confirming experiences with other occupational communities and my hunches about its applicability to other types of work organizations, my framework for understanding the persistence and transformation of intemperate drinking cultures requires further empirical validation. Several questions need to be addressed: First, are crises a necessary part of the model, or is it sufficient to have a champion for temperance in order for the transformation process to occur? Second, if crises are a necessary part of the process, what types of crises prompt occupational communities to reevaluate their intemperate drinking rituals? Must it always be, as in the sandhogs' case, an economic threat to the survival of the community, or are there other types of crises that also prompt such reevaluation? Third, must the indigenous leader who champions temperance be a member of AA or can he or she be simply a sober occupational member who feels committed to the temperance ethic? If non-AAs are able to play the champion role, do they also experience a sense of calling in this avocation? If so, how does this sense of calling develop?

Fourth, is AA's twelve-step program the only process available for converting intemperate drinkers into carriers of the new ethic of temperance? If not, what other transformation processes exist? Fifth, once the transformation process is underway, is it inevitable that the occupational intemperate drinking culture will be transformed into one of temperance? If not, what factors are likely to derail the process? What are the social consequences of derailment for the occupational community generally and those members who feel called to sobriety in particular? Sixth, what role do generations play in the transformation of intemperate drinking cultures? Are occupational communities composed of predominantly young workers more likely than communities composed of older workers to develop intemperate drinking cultures? As members of occupational communities age, are they more likely to embrace a temperance ethic, making it more likely that intemperate drinking cultures will be transformed? Empirical answers to such questions would clarify the framework's generalizability for understanding the transformation of other intemperate occupational drinking cultures.

References

Abbott, Andrew. 1988. *The System of Professions*. Chicago: University of Chicago Press.

AFL-CIO. 1993. *Helping to Overcome Addiction: A Union Representative's Guide for Dealing with Substance Abuse*. Booklet. Washington, D.C.: AFL-CIO.

Alcoholics Anonymous. 1955, 1990. *Alcoholics Anonymous*. New York: Alcoholics Anonymous World Service.

Alexander, Jeffrey C., ed. 1990. *Durkheimian Sociology: Cultural Studies*. Cambridge: Cambridge University Press.

Alexander, Jeffrey C., and Steven Seidman. 1990. *Culture and Society: Contemporary Debates*. New York: Cambridge University Press.

Ames, Genevieve. 1993. Research and Strategies for the Primary Prevention of Workplace Alcohol Problems. *Alcohol Health and Research World* 17(1): 19–27.

Ames, Genevieve M., and William Delaney. 1992. Minimization of Workplace Alcohol Problems: The Supervisor's Role. *Alcoholism Clinical and Experimental Research* 16(2): 180–89.

Ames, Genevieve M., William Delaney, and Craig R. Janes. 1992. Obstacles to Effective Alcohol Policy in the Workplace. *British Journal of Addiction* 87(7): 91–105.

Ames, Genevieve M., and Craig R. Janes. 1987. Heavy and Problem Drinking in an American Blue-Collar Population. *Social Sciences and Medicine* 25: 949–60.

123

Andrews, Florence K., Wendy E. Watkins, and Ronald L. Cosper. 1983. Alcohol and Occupational Cultures: The Social Context of Drinking among Members of Three Professions. Paper presented at Annual Meeting of American Sociological Association, Detroit, Mich.

Antze, Paul. 1987. Symbolic Action in Alcoholics Anonymous. In *Constructive Drinking*, edited by Mary Douglas. Cambridge: Cambridge University Press.

Apostolov, Miladin. 1971. Some Sociological Aspects of Alcohol Consumption and Alcoholism among Miners. *Sotsiologicheski Problem* 3(6): 73–84.

Bacharach, Samuel B., Peter B. Bamberger, and William J. Sonnenstuhl. 1994. *Member Assistance Programs: The Role of Labor in the Prevention and Treatment of Substance Abuse*. Ithaca, N.Y.: ILR Press.

Bacon, Selden D. 1945. Alcohol and Complex Society. *Alcohol, Science and Society*. New Haven, Conn.: Journal of Studies on Alcohol.

Bales, Robert F. 1946. Cultural Differences in Rates of Alcoholism. *Quarterly Journal of Studies on Alcohol* 6: 480–99.

Barley, Stephen R. 1983. The Semiotics of Funeral Work. *Urban Life* 12: 3–33.

Barnes, G. M., and M. Russell. 1977. *Drinking Patterns among Adults in New York State: A Descriptive Analysis of the Sociodemographic Correlates of Drinking*. Buffalo, N.Y.: Research Institute on Alcoholism.

Bateson, Gregory. 1971. The Cybernetics of "Self": A Theory of Alcoholism. *Psychiatry* 34(1): 1–18.

Baumohl, Jim, and Robin Room. 1987. Inebriety, Doctors, and the State: Alcoholism Treatment Institutions before 1940. In *Recent Developments in Alcoholism*. Vol. 5, edited by Marc Galanter. New York: Plenum.

Blocker, Jack S., Jr. 1989. *American Temperance Movements: Cycles of Reform*. Boston: Twayne Publishers.

Blum, Terry C., and Paul M. Roman. 1989. Employee Assistance Programs and Human Resources Management. *Research in Personnel and Human Resources Management* 7: 259–312.

Blum, Terry C., Paul M. Roman, and D. H. Tootle. 1988. The Emergence of an Occupation. *Work and Occupations* 15(1): 96–114.

Blumberg, Leonard U. 1991. *Beware the First Drink: The Washington Temperance Movement and Alcoholics Anonymous*. Seattle: Glen Abbey Books.

Blumer, Herbert. 1969. *Symbolic Interactionism*. Englewood Cliffs, N.J.: Prentice Hall.

Bogdan, Robert, and Steven J. Taylor. 1975. *Introduction to Qualitative Research Methods*. New York: John Wiley and Sons.

Braithwaite, John. 1989. *Crime, Shame, and Reintegration*. New York: Cambridge University Press.

Brandes, Stuart D. 1970. *American Welfare Capitalism*. Chicago: University of Chicago Press.

Bray, R. M., M. E. Marsden, J. V. Rachal, and M. R. Peterson. 1990. Alcohol and Drug Use in the Military Workplace: Findings from the 1988 Worldwide Survey. In *Drugs in the Workplace*, edited by S. W. Gust et al. National Institute of Drug Abuse Monograph 100. Volume 2. Washington D.C.: U.S. Government Printing Office.

Brenner, Harvey M. 1973. *Mental Illness and the Economy*. Cambridge: Harvard University Press.

————. 1975. Trends in Alcohol Consumption and Associated Illnesses: Some Effects of Economic Changes. *American Journal of Public Health* 65(12): 1279–92.

Bresard, M., and C. Gomberaux. 1962. Enquete sur la consommation des boissons aupres des mineurs du Basin de la Loire. *Bulletin of Institution of National Hygiene* 17: 217–65.

Bryant, Clifton D. 1974. Olive-Drab Drunks and G.I. Junkies: Alcohol and Narcotic Addiction in the U.S. Military. In *Deviant Behavior: Occupational and Organizational Bases*, edited by Clifton D. Bryant. Chicago: Rand McNally.

Charon, Joel M. 1992. *Symbolic Interactionism*. Englewood Cliffs, N.J.: Prentice Hall.

Clawson, Mary Ann. 1989. *Constructing Brotherhood*. Princeton: Princeton University Press.

Cohen, Anthony P. 1985. *The Symbolic Construction of Community*. London: Tavistock Publications.

Collins, Randall. 1988. *Theoretical Sociology*. New York: Harcourt Brace Jovanovich.

Collison, Dan. 1994. Profile of the Sandhogs of New York. Broadcast. *All Things Considered*. National Public Radio, 2 February 1994.

Conrad, Peter, and Joseph W. Schneider. 1992. *Deviance and Medicalization: From Badness to Sickness*. 2d. ed. Philadelphia: Temple University Press.

Conroy, David W. 1991. Puritans in Taverns: Law and Popular Culture in Colonial Massachusetts, 1630–1720. In *Drinking: Behavior and Belief in Modern History*, edited by Susanna Barrows and Robin Room. Berkeley: University of California Press.

Cosper, Ronald. 1979. Drinking as Conformity: A Critique of Sociological Literature and Occupational Differences in Drinking. *Journal of Studies on Alcohol* 40: 868–91.

Cottrell, W. Fred. 1934. Of Time and the Railroader. *American Sociological Review* 4:190–98.

————. 1940. *The Railroader*. Stanford: Stanford University Press.

Crane, Diana. 1994. *The Sociology of Culture*. Cambridge, Eng.: Blackwell.

Deal, Terrence E., and Allen A. Kennedy. 1982. *Corporate Cultures*. Reading, Mass.: Addison-Wesley.

Delaney, Paul E. 1983. *Sandhogs: A History of the Tunnel Workers of New York.* New York: Longfield Press.

Delaney, William, and Genevieve Ames. 1993. Shop Steward Handling of Alcohol-Related Problems. *Addiction* 88: 1205–14.

Denenberg, Tia S., and Richard V. Denenberg. 1991. *Alcohol and Other Drugs: Issues in Arbitration.* Washington, D.C.: Bureau of National Affairs.

Dennis, Norman, Fernando Henriques, and Clifford Slaughter. 1969. *Coal Is Our Life.* London: Tavistock Publications.

Denzin, Norman K. 1987a. *The Alcoholic Self.* Newbury Park, Calif.: Sage Publications.

———. 1987b. *The Recovering Alcoholic.* Newbury Park, Calif.: Sage Publications.

DiMaggio, Paul J., and Walter W. Powell. 1983. The Iron Cage Revisited: Institutional Isomorphism and Collective Rationality in Organizational Fields. *American Sociological Review* 48 (April): 147–60.

Douglas, Mary. 1970. *Natural Symbols.* London: Crescent Press.

Douglas, Mary, ed. 1987. *Constructive Drinking: Perspectives on Drink from Anthropology.* Cambridge: Cambridge University Press.

Douglas, Mary, and Baron Isherwood. 1980. *The World of Goods: Towards an Anthropology of Consumption.* New York: Basic Books.

Ducker, James H. 1983. *Men of the Steel Rails: Workers on the Atchison, Topeka, & Santa Fe Railroad, 1869–1900.* Lincoln: University of Nebraska Press.

Duis, Perry. 1983. *The Saloon: Public Drinking in Chicago and Boston, 1880–1920.* Urbana: University of Illinois Press.

Durkheim, Emile. [1912] 1954. *The Elementary Forms of the Religious Life.* Reprint. New York: Free Press.

Eichler, Stephen, Clifford M. Goldberg, Louise E. Kier, and John P. Allen. 1988. *Operation:RedBlock.* Rockville, Md.: U.S. Department of Transportation.

Ellis, Albert, and E. Schoenfeld. 1990. Divine Intervention and Treatment of Chemical Dependency. *Journal of Substance Abuse* 2: 459–68.

Ellis, Albert, and Emmett Velten. 1992. *When AA Doesn't Work for You: Rational Steps to Quitting Alcohol.* Fort Lee, N.J.: Barricade Books.

Emerson, Robert M., and Sheldon M. Messinger. 1977. The Micro-Politics of Trouble. *Social Problems* 25: 121–34.

Engelmann, Larry. 1979. Organized Thirst: The Story of Repeal in Michigan. In *Alcohol, Reform and Society,* edited by Jack S. Blocker, Jr. Westport, Conn.: Greenwood Press.

Erikson, Kai T. 1966. *Wayward Puritans.* New York: John Wiley and Sons.

Fennell, M. L., M. B. Rodin, and G. K. Kantor. 1981. Problems in the Work Setting: Drinking and Reasons for Drinking. *Social Forces* 60: 114–32.

Field, Peter B. 1962. A New Cross-Cultural Study of Drunkenness. In *Society, Culture, and Drinking Patterns,* edited by D. J. Pittman and C. R. Snyder. Carbondale: Southern Illinois University Press.

Fillmore, Kaye Middleton. 1990. Occupational Drinking Subcultures: An Exploratory Epidemiological Study. In *Alcohol Problem Intervention in the Workplace*, edited by P. M. Roman. Westport, Conn.: Quorum Books.

Fitzpatrick, John S. 1980. Adapting to Danger. *Sociology of Work and Occupations* 7(2): 131–58.

Ford, Leigh A. 1989. Fetching Good Out of Evil in AA: A Bormannean Fantasy Theme Analysis of the Big Book of Alcoholics Anonymous. *Communication Quarterly* 37(1): 1–15.

Freidson, Eliot. 1982. Occupational Autonomy and Labor Market Shelters. In *Varieties of Work*, edited by Phyllis L. Stewart and Muriel G. Cantor. Beverly Hills, Calif.: Sage Publications.

Frost, Peter J., Larry F. Moore, Meryl Reis Louis, Carl C. Lundberg, and Joanne Martin. 1991. *Reframing Organizational Culture*. Newbury Park, Calif.: Sage Publications.

Gamson, William, Bruce Fireman, and Steven Rytina. 1982. *Encounters with Unjust Authority*. Homewood, Ill.: Dorsey.

Gamst, Frederick C. 1980. *The Hogshead*. New York: Holt, Rinehart and Winston.

———. 1989. The Concept of Organizational and Corporate Culture: An Ethnological View. *Anthropology of Work Review* 10(3): 12–19.

Geertz, Clifford. 1973. *The Interpretation of Cultures*. New York: Basic Books.

Geist, William E. 1985. The Sandhogs Hole Through in Water Tunnel. *New York Times*, 13 February: A1.

Gellman, Irving P. 1964. *The Sober Alcoholic: An Organizational Analysis of Alcoholics Anonymous*. New Haven, Conn.: College and University Press.

Glaser, Barney, and Anselm Strauss. 1967. *The Discovery of Grounded Theory*. Chicago: Aldine.

Gluckman, Max. 1963. Gossip and Scandal. *Current Anthropology* 4(3): 307–16.

Goffman, Erving. 1974. *Frame Analysis*. New York: Harper and Row.

Goldman, Harvey. 1988. *Max Weber and Thomas Mann: Calling and the Shaping of Self*. Berkeley: University of California Press.

Goodman, Paul S., and Robert S. Atkin. 1984. *Coal Miners' Opinions about Employee Assistance Programs*. Report to Bureau of Mines, U.S. Department of the Interior. Carnegie Mellon University, Pittsburgh, Pa.

Gouldner, Alvin. 1954. *Patterns of Industrial Bureaucracy*. Glencoe, Ill.: Free Press.

Gritzer, Glenn, and Arnold Arluke. 1985. *The Making of Rehabilitation: A Political Economy of Medical Specialization*. Berkeley: University of California Press.

Gusfield, Joseph. 1975. *Community: A Critical Response*. New York: Harper and Row.

———. 1991. Benevolent Repression: Popular Culture, Social Structure, and the Control of Drinking. In *Drinking Behavior and Belief in Modern History*, edited by Susanna Barrows and Robin Room. Berkeley: University of California Press.

Gutman, Herbert G. 1976. *Work, Culture, and Society in Industrializing America*. New York: Alfred A. Knopf.

Haas, Jack. 1977. Learning Real Feelings: A Study of High Steel Ironworkers' Reactions to Fear and Danger. *Sociology of Work and Occupations* 4(2): 147–70.

Hall, T. 1990. New Way to Treat Alcoholism Discards Spiritualism of AA. *The New York Times*, 24 December: 1, 46.

Hamill, Pete. 1994. *A Drinking Life: A Memoir*. Boston: Little, Brown.

Hamper, Ben. 1991. *Rivethead: Tales from the Assembly Line*. New York: Warner Books.

Harris, Michael, and Mary L. Fennell. 1988. A Multivariate Model of Job Stress and Alcohol Abuse. *Sociological Quarterly* 29: 391–406.

Hewitt, John P. 1989. *Dilemmas of the American Self*. Philadelphia: Temple University Press.

Hill, Stephen. 1981. *Competition and Control at Work: The New Industrial Sociology*. Cambridge: MIT Press.

Hitchcock, Lyman C., and Mark S. Sanders. 1976. *A Survey of Drug and Alcohol Abuse Counseling Programs in the Railroad Industry*. Crane, Ind.: Naval Weapons Support Center.

Hodge, Robert W., Paul M. Siegel, and Peter H. Rossi. 1972. Occupational Prestige in the United States: 1925–1963. In *The Impact of Social Class*, edited by P. Blumberg. New York: Crowell.

Holbrook, Stewart H. 1947. *The Story of American Railroads*. New York: Crown Publishers.

Horton, Donald. 1945. Alcohol Use in Primitive Societies. In *Alcohol, Science, and Society*. New Haven, Conn.: Quarterly Journal of Studies in Alcohol.

Hughes, Everett. 1958. *Men and Their Work*. Glencoe, Ill.: Free Press.

Jacobs, James B., and Lynn Zimmer. 1991. Drug Treatment and Workplace Drug Testing: Politics, Symbolism, and Organizational Dilemmas. *Behavioral Sciences and the Law* 9:345–60.

Jacobson, George R., and Donald Lindsay. 1980. Screening for Alcohol Problems among the Unemployed. In *Recent Advances in Research and Treatment*. Vol. 3, edited by M. Galanter. New York: Grune and Stratton.

Janes, Craig R., and Genevieve M. Ames. 1989. Men, Blue-Collar Work and Drinking: Alcohol Use in an Industrial Subculture. *Culture, Medicine and Psychiatry* 13: 245.

Johnson, Leroy. 1981. Union Responses to Alcoholism. *Journal of Drug Issues* 11: 263–77.

Johnson, Paul. 1978. *A Shopkeeper's Millennium: Society and Revivals in Rochester, N.Y., 1815–1837*. New York: Hill and Wang.

Jones, Charisse. 1993. Six or Seven Seconds, Then Clinging to Hope. *New York Times*, 25 November: B3.

Jones, Robert K. 1970. Sectarian Characteristics of Alcoholics Anonymous. *Sociology* 4(2): 181–95.

Kranzberg, Melvin, and Joseph Gies. 1975. *By the Sweat of Thy Brow*. New York: G. P. Putnam and Sons.

Kunda, Gideon. 1992. *Engineering Culture*. Philadelphia: Temple University Press.

Kurtz, Ernest. 1979. *Not God: A History of Alcoholics Anonymous*. Center City, Minn.: Hazelden Educational Services.

Kyvig, David E. 1979. *Repealing National Prohibition*. Chicago: University of Chicago Press.

Lantz, Herman R. 1958. *People of Coal Town*. New York: Columbia University Press.

Leach, B., and J. L. Norris. 1977. Factors in the Development of Alcoholics Anonymous. In *Biology of Alcoholism*. Vol. 5. *Treatment and Rehabilitation of the Chronic Alcoholic*, edited by B. Kissin and H. Begleiter. New York: Plenum Press.

LeMasters, E. E. 1975. *Blue-Collar Aristocrats: Life Styles at a Working Class Tavern*. Madison: University of Wisconsin Press.

Lender, Mark Edward, and James Kirby Martin. 1987. *Drinking in America*. New York: Free Press.

Levine, Harry G. 1989. Introduction. In *Profits, Power and Prohibition*, by John J. Rumbarger. Albany: State University of New York.

Levine, Harry G., and Craig Reinarman. 1993. From Prohibition to Regulation: Lessons from Alcohol Policy for Drug Use. In *Drug Policy: Illicit Drugs in a Free Society*, edited by Ronald Bayer and Gerald M. Oppenheimer. New York: Cambridge University Press.

Lewin, Kurt. 1947. Group Decision and Social Change. In *Readings in Social Psychology*, edited by T. Newcomb and E. Hartley. New York: Holt, Rinehart, and Winston.

Licht, Walter. 1983. *Working for the Railroad*. Princeton: Princeton University Press.

Linsky, Arnold S., John P. Colby, Jr., and Murray A. Straus. 1991. Stress, Drinking Culture, and Alcohol Problems: A Partial Test of Bales' Theory. In *Society, Culture, and Drinking Patterns Re-examined*, edited by D. J. Pittman and H. R. White. New Brunswick, N.J.: Rutgers Center for Alcohol Studies.

Lucas, Rex A. 1969. *Men in Crisis*. New York: Basic Books.

Lukes, Steven. 1975. Political Ritual and Social Integration. *Sociology* 9: 289–308.

Lurie, N. O. 1979. The World's Oldest On-going Protest Demonstration: North American Indian Drinking Patterns. In *Beliefs, Behaviors, and Alcoholic Beverages*, edited by M. Marshall. Ann Arbor: University of Michigan Press.

McAdam, Doug, John D. McCarthy, and Mayer N. Zald. 1988. Social Movements. In *Handbook of Sociology*, edited by Neil Smelser. Newbury Park, Calif.: Sage Publications.

McAdam, Doug, and Ronnelle Paulsen. 1993. Specifying the Relationship between Social Ties and Activism. *American Journal of Sociology* 99(3): 640–67.

McCarl, Robert S. 1984. You've Come a Long Way and Now This Is Your Retirement. *Journal of American Folklore Quarterly* 97: 49–67.

MacKinnon, Neil J. 1994. *Symbolic Interaction as Affect Control*. Albany: State University of New York.

Mannello, Thomas A., and F. James Seaman. 1979. *Prevalence, Costs, and Handling of Drinking Problems on Seven Railroads*. Final Report. Washington, D.C.: University Research Corp.

Mars, Gerald. 1987. Longshore Drinking, Economic Security and Union Politics in Newfoundland. In *Constructive Drinking*, edited by M. Douglas. Cambridge: Cambridge University Press.

Martin, Jack K., Terry C. Blum, and Paul M. Roman. 1992. Drinking to Cope and Self-Medication: Characteristics of Jobs in Relation to Workers' Drinking Behavior. *Journal of Organizational Behavior* 13: 55–71.

Martin, Joanne. 1992. *Cultures in Organizations*. New York: Oxford University Press.

Mather, Cotton. [1708] 1940. Sober Consideration on a Growing Flood of Iniquity. In *Cotton Mather: A Bibliography of His Works*, edited by T. J. Holmes. Vol. 3. Cambridge: Harvard University Press.

Mather, Increase. [1673] 1931. "Wo to Drunkards." In *Increase Mather: A Bibliography of His Works*, edited by T. J. Holmes. Vol. 2. Cambridge: Harvard University Press.

Maxwell, Milton A. 1950. The Washingtonian Movement. *Quarterly Journal of Alcohol Studies* 11: 410–51.

———. 1984. *The Alcoholics Anonymous Experience: A Close-Up View for Professionals*. New York: McGraw-Hill.

Meyer, John W., and Brian Rowan. 1977. Institutionalized Organizations: Formal Structure as Myth and Ceremony. *American Journal of Sociology* 83 (September): 340–63.

Miller, M., and J. Van Maanen. 1982. Getting into Fishing: Social Identities of Fishermen. *Urban Life* 11(1): 27–54.

Miller, William R., and Ernest Kurtz. 1994. Models of Alcoholism Used in Treatment: Contrasting AA and Other Perspectives with Which It Is Often Confused. *Journal of Studies on Alcohol* 55: 159–66.

Moore, Sally F., and Barbara G. Myerhoff. 1977. Secular Ritual: Forms and Meaning. In *Secular Ritual*, edited by Sally F. Moore and Barbara G. Myeroff. Amsterdam: Van Gorcum.

Nash, June C. 1979. *We Eat the Mines*. New York: Columbia University Press.

National Institute of Medicine. 1990. *Broadening the Base of Treatment for Alcohol Problems*. Washington, D.C.: NIM.

Niederhoffer, A., and E. Niederhoffer. 1978. *The Policy Family*. Lexington, Mass.: D. C. Heath.

Ogborne, Alan, and Andrew Bornet. 1982. Abstinence and Abusive Drinking among Affiliates of Alcoholics Anonymous: Are These the Only Alternatives? *Addictive Behaviors* 7: 199–202.

Ojesjo, Leif. 1980. The Relationship to Alcoholism of Occupation, Class, and Employment. *Journal of Occupational Medicine* 22(10): 657–66.

O'Toole, James. 1974. *Work in America*. Washington, D.C.: U.S. Department of Health, Education and Welfare.

Parker, Douglas A., and Thomas C. Harford. 1992. The Epidemiology of Alcohol Consumption and Dependence across Occupations in the United States. *Alcohol, Health and Research World* 16(2): 97–105.

Parsons, Talcott. 1937. *The Structure of Social Action*. New York: McGraw-Hill.

———. 1951. *The Social System*. Glencoe, Ill.: Free Press.

Pilcher, William W. 1972. *The Portland Longshoremen*. New York: Holt, Rinehart and Winston.

Poleksic, J. 1969. Alocholism and the Critical Occupations. *Alkoholizam* 9(3): 41–51. Abstract 1971. *Quarterly Journal of Studies on Alcohol* 32(2): 556.

Powers, Madelon. 1991. Decay from Within: The Inevitable Doom of the American Saloon. In *Drinking: Behavior and Belief in Modern History*, edited by S. Barrows and R. Room. Berkeley: University of California Press.

Pursch, Jack A. 1976. From Quonset Hut to Naval Hospital. *Journal of Studies on Alcohol* 37: 1655–65.

Reinhardt, Richard. 1970. *Workin' on the Railroad*. Palo Alto, Calif.: American West Publishing Company.

Riemer, Jeffery R. 1979. *Hard Hats: The Work World of Construction Workers*. Beverly Hills, Calif.: Sage Publications.

———. 1982. Worker Autonomy in the Skilled Building Trades. In *Varieties of Work*, edited by P. L. Stewart and M. G. Cantor. Beverly Hills, Calif.: Sage Publications.

Robinson, D. 1979. *Talking Out of Alcoholism: The Self-Help Process of Alcoholics Anonymous*. Baltimore: University Park Press.

Roman, Paul M. 1981. Job Characteristics and the Identification of Deviant Drinking. *Journal of Drug Issues* 11: 357–64.

———. 1982. Employee Assistance Programs in Major Corporations in 1979. *Prevention, Intervention, and Treatment: Concerns and Models*. Rockville, Md.: U.S. Department of Health and Human Services.

Roman, Paul M., and Harrison M. Trice. 1970. The Development of Deviant Drinking Behavior. *Archives of Environmental Health* 20: 424–35.

Rorabaugh, W. J. 1979. *The Alcoholic Republic.* New York: Oxford University Press.

Rosenzweig, Roy. 1983. *Eight Hours for What We Will.* New York: Oxford University Press.

Roy, Donald. 1960. "Banana Time": Job Satisfaction and Informal Interaction. *Human Organization* 18: 158–69.

Rudy, David R. 1986. *Becoming Alcoholic: Alcoholics Anonymous and the Reality of Alcoholism.* Carbondale, Ill.: Southern Illinois University Press.

Rumbarger, John J. 1989. *Profits, Power, and Prohibition.* Albany: SUNY Press.

Runcie, John F. 1980. By Days I Make the Cars. *Harvard Business Review* 58 (May/June): 106–15.

———. 1988. Deviant Behavior: Achieving Autonomy in a Machine-Paced Environment. In *Inside Organizations,* edited by Michael Owen Jones, Michael Dane Moore, and Richard Christopher Snyder. Newbury Park, Calif.: Sage Publications.

Rush, Benjamin. [1784] 1943. An Inquiry into the Effects of Ardent Spirits Upon the Human Body and Mind. *Quarterly Journal of Studies on Alcohol* 4:2 324–41.

Salaman, Graeme. 1974. *Community and Occupation: An Exploration of Work/Leisure Relationships.* Cambridge: Cambridge University Press.

———. 1986. *Working.* London: Tavistock Publications.

Schein, Edgar H. 1985. *Organizational Culture and Leadership.* San Francisco: Jossey-Bass.

Schwartz, Howard, and Jerry Jacobs. 1979. *Qualitative Sociology.* New York: Free Press.

Searle-Chatterjee, Mary. 1979. The Polluted Identity of Work. In *Social Anthropology of Work,* edited by S. Waldman. New York: Academic Press.

Seidman, J., J. London, B. Karsh, and D. L. Tagliacozzo. 1958. *The Worker Views His Union.* Chicago: University of Chicago Press.

Shore, Elsie R. 1985a. Alcohol Consumption among Managers and Professionals. *Journal of Studies on Alcohol* 46: 153–56.

———. 1985b. Norms Regarding Drinking Behavior in the Business Environment. *Journal of Social Psychology* 125: 735–41.

Silver, Marc L. 1986. *Under Construction.* Albany: State University of New York Press.

Smith, Dennis. 1972. *Report from Engine Company Eighty-Two.* New York: Dutton.

Snow, David A., E. Burke Rochford, Jr., Steven K. Worden, and Robert Benford. 1986. Frame Alignment Processes, Micromobilization, and Movement Participation. *American Sociological Review* 51: 464–81.

Sonnenstuhl, William J. 1986. *Inside an Emotional Health Program.* Ithaca, N.Y.: ILR Press.

————. 1990. Help-Seeking and the Helping Processes within the Workplace: Assisting Alcoholic and Other Troubled Employees. In *Alcohol Problem Intervention in the Workplace,* edited by Paul M. Roman. Westport, Conn.: Quorum Books.

Sonnenstuhl, William J., and Harrison M. Trice. 1987. The Social Construction of Alcohol Problems in a Union's Peer Counseling Program. *Journal of Drug Issues* 17(3): 223–54.

————. 1991. Organizations and Types of Occupational Communities. In *Research in the Sociology of Organizations,* edited by Samuel B. Bacharach. Vol. 9. Greenwich, Conn.: JAI Press.

Spradley, James. 1979. *The Ethnographic Interview.* New York: Holt, Rinehart, and Winston.

Staudenmeier, William J., Jr. 1985. Alcohol and the Workplace: A Study of Social Policy in a Changing America. Ph.D. dis., Washington University.

Stinchcombe, Arthur L. 1959. Bureaucratic and Craft Administration of Production. *Administrative Science Quarterly* 4 (September): 3–21.

Stinson, Fredrick S., Samar Fara DeBakey, and Rebecca A. Steffens. 1992. Prevalence of DSM-III-R Alcohol Abuse and/or Dependence among Selected Occupations: United States, 1988. *Alcohol, Health and Research World* 16(2): 165–72.

Stivers, Richard. 1985. Historical Meanings of Irish-American Drinking. In *American Experience with Alcohol,* edited by Linda Bennett and G. M. Ames. New York: Plenum Press.

Straus, Robert. 1975. Reconceptualizing Social Problems in Light of Scholarly Advances. In *Social Policy and Sociology,* edited by N. Demerath, O. Larsen, and K. Schuessler. New York: Academic Press.

Strauss, Anselm. 1987. *Qualitative Analysis for Social Scientists.* New York: Cambridge University Press.

Strauss, Anselm, and Juliet Corbin. 1990. *Basics of Qualitative Research.* Newbury Park, Calif.: Sage Publications.

Swindler, Ann. 1986. Culture in Action: Symbols and Strategies. *American Sociological Review* 51: 273–86.

Taussig, Michael T. 1980. *The Devil and Commodity Fetishism in South America.* Chapel Hill: University of North Carolina Press.

Trice, Harrison M. 1957. A Study of the Process of Affiliation with Alcoholics Anonymous. *Quarterly Journal of Studies on Alcohol* 18: 39–54.

————. 1965a. Alcoholic Employees: A Comparison of Psychotic, Neurotic and "Normal" Personnel. *Journal of Occupational Medicine* 7: 79–98.

————. 1965b. Reaction of Supervisors to Emotionally Disturbed Employees. *Journal of Occupational Medicine* 7: 77–108.

————. 1993. *Occupational Subcultures in the Workplace.* Ithaca, N.Y.: ILR Press.

Trice, Harrison M., and Janice M. Beyer. 1982. A Study of Union-Management Cooperation in a Long-Standing Alcoholism Program. *Contemporary Drug Problems* 11: 295–317.

———. 1984. Employee Assistance Programs. In *Research in Community Mental Health,* edited by James R. Greenberg. Vol. 4. Greenwich, Conn.: JAI Press.

———. 1991. Cultural Leadership in Organizations. *Organization Science* 2(2): 149–69.

———. 1993. *The Cultures of Work Organizations.* Englewood Cliffs, N.J.: Prentice Hall.

Trice, Harrison M., Janice M. Beyer, and Cynthia Coppess. 1981. Sowing Seeds of Change. *Journal of Drug Issues* 11: 311–36.

Trice, Harrison M., Richard E. Hunt, Janice M. Beyer. 1981. Alcoholism Programs in Unionized Work Settings. *Journal of Drug Issues* 7(2): 103–15.

Trice, Harrison M., and Paul M. Roman. 1970a. Delabeling, Relabeling, and Alcoholics Anonymous. *Social Problems* 17: 468–80.

———. 1970b. Sociopsychological Predictors of Affiliation with Alcoholics Anonymous. *Social Psychiatry* 5: 51–59.

———. 1972. *Spirits and Demons at Work.* Ithaca, N.Y.: ILR Press.

Trice, Harrison M., and Mona Schonbrunn. 1981. A History of Job-Based Alcoholism Programs: 1900–1955. *Journal of Drug Issues* 11: 171–98.

Trice, Harrison M., and William J. Staudenmeier, Jr. 1989. A Socio-Cultural History of Alcoholics Anonymous. In *Recent Developments in Alcoholism,* edited by Marc Galanter. Vol. 7. New York: Plenum Press.

Trimpey, Jack. 1989. *The Small Book: A Revolutionary Alternative for Overcoming Alcohol and Other Drug Dependence.* New York: Delacorte Press.

Turner, Victor W. 1969. *The Ritual Process: Structure and Anti-Structure.* Chicago: Aldine.

Tyrrell, Ian. 1979. *Sobering Up: From Temperance to Prohibition in Antebellum America, 1800–1860.* Westport, Conn.: Greenwood Press.

Van Gennep, Arnold. [1908] 1960. *The Rites of Passage.* Reprint. Chicago: University of Chicago Press.

Van Maanen, John. 1973. Observations on the Making of Policemen. *Human Organization* 32: 407–18.

———. 1980. Beyond Account: The Personal Impacts of Police Shootings. *The Annals of the American Academy of Political and Social Science* 451(3): 145–56.

Van Maanen, John, and Stephen R. Barley. 1984. Occupational Communities: Culture and Control in Organizations. *Research in Organizational Behavior* 6: 287–365.

Van Maanen, John, and Edgar H. Schein. 1979. Toward a Theory of Organizational Socialization. In *Research in Organizational Behavior,* edited by Barry M. Straw. Vol. 1. Greenwich, Conn.: JAI Press.

Vaught, Charles, and David L. Smith. 1980. Incorporation and Mechanical Solidarity in an Underground Coal Mine. *Sociology of Work and Occupations* 7(2): 159–87.

Walsh, Diana Chapman, Ralph W. Higson, Daniel M. Merrigan, Suzette Morelock Levenson, L. Adrienne Cupples, and Timothy Heeren. 1992. A Randomized Trial of Alternative Treatments for Problem-Drinking Employees: Study Design, Major Findings, and Lessons for Worksite Research. *Journal of Employee Assistance Research* 1(1): 63–82.

Wardell, Mark. 1992. Changing Organizational Forms: From the Bottom Up. In *Rethinking Organization: New Directions in Organizational Analysis*, edited by Michael Reed and Michael Hughes. Newbury Park, Calif.: Sage Publications.

Warner, Jessica. 1994. "Resolv'd to Drink No More": Addiction as a Preindustrial Construct. *Journal of Studies on Alcohol* 55: 685–91.

Weber, Max. [1905] 1958. *The Protestant Ethic and the Spirit of Capitalism*, Reprint. New York: Scribner.

———. [1919] 1958a. Science as a Vocation. In *From Max Weber*, edited by Hans Gerth and C. Wright Mills. Oxford: Oxford University Press.

———. [1919] 1958b. Politics as a Vocation. In *From Max Weber*, edited by Hans Gerth and C. Wright Mills. Oxford: Oxford University Press.

———. [1922] 1968. *Economy and Society*. Berkeley: University of California Press.

West, Major Louis Jolyon, and Master Sergeant William H. Swegan. 1956. An Approach to Alcoholism in the Military Service. *American Journal of Psychiatry* 112: 1004–14.

Whitley, Oliver R. 1977. Life with Alcoholics Anonymous: The Methodist Class Meeting as a Paradigm. *Journal of Studies on Alcohol* 138: 831–48.

Whyte, William Foote. 1984. *Learning from the Field*. Beverly Hills, Calif.: Sage Publications.

Wilentz, Sean. 1985. *Chants Democratic*. New York: Oxford University Press.

Wuthnow, Robert. 1987. *Meaning and Moral Order: Explorations in Cultural Analysis*. Berkeley: University of California Press.

Zucker, Lynne G. 1991. The Role of Institutionalization in Cultural Persistence. In *The New Institutionalism in Ogranizational Analysis*, edited by Walter W. Powell and Paul J. DiMaggio. Chicago: University of Chicago Press.

Index